Smart, Fast, Efficient:

The New Principal's Guide to Success

Leanna Stohr Isaacson, PhD

EYE ON EDUCATION
6 DEPOT WAY WEST, SUITE 106
LARCHMONT, NY 10538
(914) 833–0551
(914) 833–0761 fax
www.eyeoneducation.com

Library of Congress Cataloging-in-Publication Data

Isaacson, Leanna Stohr, 1939-
Smart, fast, efficient : the new principal's guide to success / Leanna Stohr Isaacson.
      p. cm.
Includes bibliographical references.
ISBN-13: 978-1-59667-016-7
ISBN-10: 1-59667-016-9
1. First year school principals--United States--Handbooks, manuals, etc. 2. School management and organization--United States--Handbooks, manuals, etc. I. Title.
LB2831.92.I83 2005
371.2'012--dc22

2005025191

10 9 8 7 6 5 4 3 2

Editorial and production services provided by
Richard H. Adin Freelance Editorial Services
52 Oakwood Blvd., Poughkeepsie, NY 12603-4112
(845-471-3566)

Also Available from EYE ON EDUCATION

What Great Principals Do Differently:
15 Things That Matter Most
Todd Whitaker

What Successful Principals Do!
169 Tips for Principals
Franzy Fleck

BRAVO Principal!
Sandra Harris

The Administrator's Guide to School Community Relations,
Second Edition
George E. Pawlas

School Leader Internship: Developing, Monitoring,
and Evaluating Your Leadership Experience, 2nd Ed.
Martin, Wright, Danzig, Flanary, and Brown

Talk It Out!
The Educator's Guide to Successful Difficult Conversations
Barbara E. Sanderson

Making the Right Decisions:
A Guide for School Leaders
Douglas J. Fiore and Chip Joseph

Dealing with Difficult Teachers, Second Edition
Todd Whitaker

Dealing with Difficult Parents
(And with Parents in Difficult Situations)
Todd Whitaker and Douglas Fiore

Elevating Student Voice:
How To Enhance Participation, Citizenship, and Leadership
Nelson Beaudoin

Stepping Outside Your Comfort Zone:
Lessons for School Leaders
Nelson Beaudoin

Great Quotes for Great Educators
Todd Whitaker and Dale Lumpa

What Great Teachers Do Differently:
14 Things That Matter Most
Todd Whitaker

20 Strategies for Collaborative School Leaders
Jane Clark Lindle

Motivating & Inspiring Teachers
The Educational Leader's Guide for Building Staff Morale
Todd Whitaker, Beth Whitaker, and Dale Lumpa

The Principal as Instructional Leader:
A Handbook for Supervisors
Sally J. Zepeda

Instructional Leadership for School Improvement
Sally J. Zepeda

Six Types of Teachers:
Recruiting, Retaining, and Mentoring the Best
Douglas J. Fiore and Todd Whitaker

Supervision Across the Content Areas
Sally J. Zepeda and R. Stewart Mayers

The ISLLC Standards in Action:
A Principal's Handbook
Carol Engler

Harnessing the Power of Resistance:
A Guide for Educators
Jared Scherz

Data Analysis for Continuous School Improvement
Victoria L. Bernhardt

Handbook on Teacher Evaluation:
Assessing and Improving Performance
James Stronge & Pamela Tucker

Acknowledgments

Special recognition must go to those who most influenced the writing of this book. To the staff of Southwood Elementary School, I owe a special debt of gratitude. Over the years, I was part of a school culture that was rich with high-quality teachers (almost one-third of the staff had achieved National Board Certification by 2005), great students, and caring, hardworking parents from 54 countries. Together, we worked through the trials, tribulations, and jubilations that occur when creating a learning community. Special appreciation goes to those who maintain a strong sense of loyalty and commitment to the vision of creating a constructivist school. I learned from them, from their openness, and from their willingness to think, solve problems, and implement effective teaching strategies.

My son Greg, a lawyer, Nationally Board Certified teacher, and chairman of the English Department at Olympia High School in Orange County, Florida, provided insight from the perspective of a high school teacher who sees secondary school issues that occur. He also reviewed this manuscript and helped to sort out the concerns and challenges that exist in schools. He has the experience of teaching in more than one state and in a variety of settings: rural, inner city, and suburban.

The real world requires the perspective of stakeholders. None served this role better than my daughter, Lara McMahon, as a parent and her son, my grandson, Destin, who attended our school. I studied our school through their eyes. Destin and his friends were comfortable collecting in my office from kindergarten through Grade 5 and openly discussed teachers, substitute teachers, and each other. I kept invisible as I listened to their views on effective teaching, homework, standardized testing, and girls. My daughter provided the parent position on school, family stress with homework, report cards, standardized testing, and encouraging high academic standards.

Everyone needs a mentor or two. My major professor, Arthur Shapiro, and his wife, Sue, served that role. They encouraged me and provided valuable insight into my research. Dr. Shapiro guided me through the process of creating a constructivist school environment. He served as a mentor to the school through his problem-solving approach. Sue Shapiro also helped us to understand the importance of identifying, accepting, and working with individual differences among the staff.

Without the insight of my principal colleagues around the country, this book would not exist. Continuous discussions concerning our administrative jobs, strategies for working with staff, problem solving how to deal with the carrot-and-stick approach to high-stakes testing, creative ideas for celebrations, and balancing our lives provided the real-world experiences identified in the following pages.

Special thanks to those who endured my continuous questioning and reflection while providing exceptional support over the years: Kim Stutsman, principal; Judy Cunningham, area superintendent; Ralph Hewitt, retired principal and educational consultant; Laurie Welch-Storch, current principal of Southwood Elementary School; Dee Frechette, teacher; Vicki Roscoe, principal; and H. Lynn Erickson, educational consultant.

Finally, I owe a tremendous dept of gratitude to publisher Bob Sickles. He encouraged me to write about what I know best—the principal's job. His patience and understanding kept me going. He helped to cement my belief that I could help the new principal with the often-untold issues that occur in the real world of school administration, particularly during the first year.

About the Author

Leanna Stohr Isaacson is a veteran educator who has worked as a teacher in several districts and at all grade levels (including exceptional education) and as a principal in both the Northwest and in the Southeast. She has studied and lived the challenges of principalship from both a rural and urban perspective in inner-city and suburban schools, high diversity, and, most recently, in a high-stakes environment.

Dr. Isaacson is a frequent presenter at national and international conferences. Most recently, her presentation topics have surrounded issues concerning the change process needed to create a total school with a common constructivist philosophy and vision.

Dr. Isaacson received her BA and MEd from the University of Montana and, in 2004, received a PhD in interdisciplinary studies (curriculum and instruction, educational leadership) from the University of South Florida. She currently serves as a visiting assistant professor in educational leadership at Stetson University in Celebration, Florida.

Preface

The 21st century began a new era in school administration. Never before have principals in urban, high-growth areas been in such short supply as veteran principals begin to retire. New principals are entering a position that is increasingly complex and highly politicized.

The terms *smart*, *fast*, and *efficient* describe the skills and talents modern administrators need to meet the ever-increasing demands on school leaders. They must have a high tolerance for the ambiguities that exist when micromanaging occurs at the district, state, and national levels. High-stakes testing adds a layer of accountability that challenges any administrator, particularly those who have limited classroom experience. This means the new leader must learn and understand all aspects of curriculum, instruction, and assessment analysis. This is no longer a task assigned specifically to someone else, primarily because the buck stops with the principal as the instructional leader.

As the leader, you will demonstrate an understanding of all aspects of the school culture and an ability to communicate the philosophy and vision of the school to all stakeholders. You will be expected to explain how teachers teach and how students will pass the tests, and you will have to meet the needs of all members of the school. All eyes will be focused on your ability to help students and teachers improve and your talent in understanding how and why students and teachers meet the expectations of the school community. As a new leader, you have been hired because you are among the best and the brightest and possess multiple talents, high motivation, and the willingness to learn for the rest of your career.

That sounds pretty overwhelming, doesn't it? It can be unless you approach each school task and issue methodically, analytically, and sensitively while working smart, fast, and efficient.

Who Should Read this Book?

This book is written for principals who are new to a school, new assistant principals, newly appointed assistants, or assistants who have acquired a new principal. A person entertaining the idea of becoming a school administrator may read this book and realize the variety of issues that are a part of the job. It is written for the administrator who is entering a school for the first time in the high-stakes arena. The very busy principal or assistant principal needs a quick read that "cuts to the chase" when there isn't time to plow through large texts of information.

This book is written for district or central office people who are responsible for supporting the newly appointed administrator or directing principal training programs. It is written as a supplemental resource for students and professors in college classes in educational leadership for new administrators. Questions for discussion appear at the end of each chapter. References for further study are found at the end of the book.

This book is not written for the seasoned master principal but for the veteran principal with an assistant who may need guidance. This book is written for the beginning administrator's appointment to a new position, even before the principal or assistant principal has met the staff for the first staff meeting. It starts by providing topics and ideas that may help to reduce the anxiety that comes with a new job. This book will help the new principal determine the sequence of tasks so that the magnitude of the job does not become unnecessarily overwhelming. It identifies strategies to efficiently and effectively lay a foundation on which to build a high-performing school.

Principals frustrated by a lack of progress within the school may find parts of this book helpful. Reading selected chapters may reveal missing pieces in the school's strategic planning.

This book is also written for the principal or assistant who receives an administrative appointment and says, "I know the stakes are high. Where do I begin?" It is a book based on real issues with honest experiences and practical applications from a common "horse sense" perspective. This is a view from the trenches.

The administrator's job looks very different once the position is obtained. Principals and assistants new to the job will reveal their feelings of being overwhelmed. Why? Because the reality of the job is rarely discussed in any detail, nor do seated principals explain their thinking as they solve problems and work their way through the complicated and off-the-wall issues that come their way. They just do what they do. However, that doesn't help a new principal or assistant understand how to do the job.

This is an era of high stakes in education when expectations for the high performance of students require high performance among administrators. A new leader needs specific, step-by-step details about what to do, when to do it, and how to do it.

You will not read another list of competencies nor find detailed explanations about what an exceptional principal does. Outstanding principals evolve; they are not born with "effective principal genes." Veteran principals would not have staying power if they had not learned to lead a school through carefully developed, organized, and rationally planned responses to both predictable and unimagined situations. This book does not focus on the end of the story, when a principal has his or her arms wrapped around the school, when teacher and student improvement has occurred, and when the philosophy and vision have become entrenched.

This book will not provide all the answers to every situation. Schools are too complex to assume that one size will fit all issues that arise. However, many common issues occur regardless of the size of the school, culture, or state and local expectations. This is a heads up that could avoid major backpedaling, inefficient use of time, unnecessary frustration, and reduce the stress on an administrator who tries to do too much, too soon, with incomplete information.

The topics are identified according to the month in which the task should be accomplished during the school year. The purpose of a month-by-month recommendation rests in the knowledge that when principals accomplish one task at a time, revisiting some tasks in greater depth throughout the year, they work smarter and more efficiently. Some tasks can wait—but which ones? The focused principal learns to develop an overview of the year's tasks and then takes them on in a scheduled plan to avoid delays, frustration, and a sense of urgency that everything must be done now.

If the ideas do not fit exactly into an administrator's immediate situation, the strategies can be adapted to most issues that develop during the first year of an administrator's appointment to the principal or assistant principal position. For example, the monthly calendar is an example of how to develop an overview of what is to come during the year. However, every school begins and ends its school year at different times. Adjust the example based on your individual district and school requirements.

Verification of Key Issues

The helpful hints and comments in this book are a result of teachers' experiences, veteran administrators' insights, and my own learning. Personal experiences were authenticated and supplemented through documentation from additional sources.

Interviews with Teachers

Qualitative research for a doctoral dissertation was conducted by interviewing teachers to determine what teaching staff consider to be the key requirements necessary for teachers and students to succeed in a constructivist environment. The information included in this book was not drawn from the research questions directly and the answers that directed the formal process, but from additional comments that were made. During focus group interviews, teachers described the necessary role principals must play in building a successful school environment. The unexpected answers provided rich insight into the expectations of teachers as they relate to their boss.

Interviews with Principals

Using the indirect comments from teachers, interviews took place with other principals. The settings were planned and unplanned, structured and unstructured. I listened to principals tell their stories. Both veteran and beginning colleagues shared experiences. We talked over long-distance phone calls to practicing principals on the West Coast from private and public schools and over e-mail, coffee, lunch, or visits in principal's offices in Orlando, Florida.

The primary focus of inquiry was the following: What is the most difficult part of the job, particularly during the first year? What seems to get in the way of principals feeling successful? What information and suggestions would be helpful?

These insightful comments provided the questions that needed answering. New leaders know the *what* part of the job requirements, but often they become frustrated with the *how* part of the job. The "how to do it" became the foundation for each chapter.

You may ask the question, "Will this book help me raise test scores?" The answer is no. However, the suggestions may provide focus points so that you and your staff can develop a thoughtful plan to raise student test scores.

How Is the Book Organized?

Chapters are organized one month at a time and will need adjustment according to your individual district and school. There is a built-in assumption that you will receive your appointment sometime near the summer. For purposes of consistency, the time frame begins with your appointment, presumably in June, and progresses through the first year on the job, month by month, so that the magnitude of the job does not become overly stressful.

If your appointment does not occur in June, begin when you accept the position and work with your adjusted time frame. In this way, you won't try to do too much too soon and become overwhelmed.

You have read the literature on what effective principals do. However, there is a huge leap from your current position, even if you are an assistant principal, to that of the leader of the school. There are *sequential tasks* to accomplish that begin at the time you believe your appointment is inevitable. By approaching each issue and task in a sequential fashion, you build the foundation for the structure of your new home.

Impatient as you may be to get going, remind yourself that you are building your dream home. Without a well-designed, carefully planned blueprint, studying and analyzing each step, the house may stand for a short time, but it won't last long if the foundation is not secured. Even before the first slab is poured, think of all the steps you must go through before the first load of cement arrives. Time and patience, methodical planning, and careful supervision will create the home that you, the contractors, and the workers build.

Even if you move into an old house and plan on remodeling, you don't walk through the door and begin tearing out a wall. (It could be a weight-bearing wall—big mistake.) You must spend time in the home, living in it a while, studying the possibilities, examining any remodeling the previous owners thought important. You have a design in mind, but you take it slowly, step by step. Remodeling is expensive, and you have a limited budget. It is worth it to take your time. Then, every decision is thoughtfully planned. Although it takes time, in the end, the house will be the one you dreamed about.

Each chapter can stand alone. If you feel you know and understand parts of the job and need no more information, or if you want a refresher on specific tasks, you may want to skip to the relevant chapters. If you are new to the position or think administration is something that may interest you, read from the beginning to the end. This may provide a clearer picture of how management and leadership skills progress throughout the year.

You will notice that some topics repeat themselves. Some tasks recycle throughout the year. The level of sophistication and purpose with which you approach each issue deepens as you become more knowledgeable and develop a clearer focus of your vision. For example, data will be analyzed many times at the beginning of your appointment when meeting with teams and individuals and when planning for next year. Each review requires more in-depth assessment of the information. Teacher observations will be different during your first observations (as a new principal, you don't know the culture or the teachers early in the year). The depth of your observation will be much greater later in the year, when you have a clearer picture of what you are looking for and to what degree.

Your purpose may become more focused, your philosophy adjusted, and your vision revised as the year progresses. After four to six months of interacting with the school community, you will have a much stronger handle on your beliefs in relation to the school. This is the time to revisit and rewrite your thoughts from the beginning of the year, when you really are pretty clueless compared to the much greater clarity you will have gained several months later.

The sequence of chapters in this book will provide detailed suggestions about ways to examine each topic as it occurs throughout the school year.

Each month is identified as a way to further delineate and illustrate ways to sequence the various tasks and issues before you.

The Appendix section contains three items to reference throughout the text: (1) an explanation of warning signs that you may be overwhelmed, and (2) statements identifying the 10 key components to keep in mind as you work your way through the school year.

How Is Each Chapter Organized?

Chapters are organized in a monthly sequence. In this way, aspiring administrators can sort and organize their jobs and determine the specific issues that must be addressed without trying to do everything at once.

- The beginning of each chapter provides an introduction.
- Identified topics contain the following explanations under key headings: *When Do I Begin?* and *What Should I Do and How Should I Do It?*
- *Short anecdotes* from principals at all levels illustrate the points made within the chapters.
- *Questions and Answers* expand on areas where the reader may need clarification.
- *Survival Tips* highlight important issues that could save the new administrator from unnecessary grief.
- The end of each chapter provides a *Summary* for the reader to pick and choose the topics of greatest interest.
- *Reflections* complete each chapter. These are intended to give the reader guided reflection or generate discussions in college classes or principal training programs.
- *Supporting literature* is located in the References section at the end of the book.

Table of Contents

1

Preparing for Your Assignment: The Journey Begins

(Two Months before School Begins)

Each of the skills and talents you need to perform successfully as a school administrator is predicated on your ability to think, analyze tasks, and solve problems. This is done in an atmosphere of congeniality, collegiality, openness, respect for the school's culture and the staff, students, and parents who work within it.

A challenge awaits you. You don't have the luxury of taking as much time as you need to learn on the job because in the current high-stakes environment, the expectation it that you will "hit the ground running." You must have a clear sense of who you are and what you want to accomplish.

You already understand the concept of moving *faster* because you grew up in the quick-paced society of the 20th century. You will become very *efficient* to accomplish the requirements of leading in the ever more complex job of school administration. Time is your most valuable commodity, and wasting it only adds to the challenge. You will learn to work smarter, not harder.

Youth is in your favor because you possess the physical and mental energy needed to maintain a rigorous schedule. The enthusiasm and motivation you bring to the job will energize those around you.

Smart, fast, and *efficient* characteristics will become your greatest strengths. Limited experiences in a variety of classroom settings and the magnitude of the job are the greatest challenges. The multitude of responsibilities both surprises and overwhelms most new principals. Guess what? You are not alone. Most new principals and assistants feel the same way. So much hits you at once.

Life before Administration

Before launching into the complexities of the job, step back and take some time to think carefully about two issues. First, reflect on your educational life before you made the career move from teacher or support person to school administrator.

Your new job is very different from your world in the classroom. As a teacher, you controlled your world. Once you closed your doors, you were in charge of everyone. Except for some intercom announcements, the only interruptions that occurred during your class were generally at your discretion. You were generally self-confident as a teacher, doing a good job, knowing your subject matter, and watching students' progress.

You had a relatively large support system in your colleagues. You often hung out together to compare notes, bounce ideas, and brainstorm with each other to figure out the best solution to concerns about your students, instruction, or assessments. Yes, you often griped about the administrator for one thing or the other.

You might have joined your circle of colleagues after school to further cement your bonds with your group. Unless you have some personal interest in a content area that is out of your field of knowledge, what and how other teachers teach was usually of minimum concern. You had your hands full with your own classes.

At some moment in time, you decided to begin the journey into school administration. The decision to enter an administrative career was not easy. Prior to making the commitment, you probably consulted family, friends, and peers who provided you with the encouragement to continue in the pursuit of your goal—becoming an assistant and then a principal. I learned that the top three reasons for changing roles in education from teacher to administrator are (1) a desire to make more money, (2) a belief that the job will provide you with a chance to make a bigger difference in education, and (3) a feeling that of being tired of teaching and a need to make a change.

Yet, in determining your personal goals, did you think carefully about the deeper issues of entering administration? What is the purpose you want to achieve as a principal? Raising test scores, helping every child improve, and repeating the school district's mission statement are a given.

Second, define your inner purpose. What is it about your inner purpose that attracts you to administration? What reasons do you give for pursuing a career in administration with excitement and enthusiasm? What talents do you possess that you will take into your new school as a leader and manager? (Cottrell, 2005). Think about your motivation and the driving forces that developed as you made the decision to enter administration. On the drive back and forth to work, when you wake up in the morning, or during any quiet time, reflect on the serious importance of knowing in your heart why you are embarking on such an important path. Talk about your reflections with your peers and your best friends so that they hear what you are thinking. A clear sense of who you are and why you are doing what you do creates a principal or assistant with a solid foundation on which to build a productive career.

Your New Life

Before you made the final leap, you and your significant other reached an agreement on the hours you will spend at work, especially during the first year or two. You discussed that even though research says most principals work a 10-hour day, in reality it's really 12 hours on a good day.

If you don't live near the school, you will probably stay at work when there are evening parent meetings or outside events such as dances, sports, and performances that you are expected to attend. This extends your work day to 12–16 hours. In addition, it is common for principals to attend weekend events such as Saturday sports events, parent-organized family days, and extracurricular activities sponsored by any number of school-approved organizations.

Your partner is prepared, if you have one. Prepare your children, if you have that responsibility. (Your dog, if you have one, will be happy to see you whenever you get home.) Everyone in your world understands the importance of your new position, and you have their support. That agreement has been reached.

You completed the arduous task of complying with district and state requirements. Educational leadership classes were completed in which you were trained to learn the list of competencies required by your state and local agencies. You were coached and passed the certification test.

You experienced excitement and anxiety when you continued through the process of meeting local requirements. This can mean anything from further testing and interviews after you met the criteria for acceptance into the administrators-in-waiting group to a single phone call of congratulations. Family and friends celebrated your accomplishments.

In larger schools, the process usually begins by becoming an assistant principal and after a period of apprenticeship, and once you have proven that you are ready, someone dubs you principal. Or, as a classroom or support teacher, you become an assistant. You became a member of the "Principal's Club" or "Assistant Principal's Club." You have watched principals at work. You know you are ready.

Generally, what skills and experiences from the real world of administration actually prepared you for the job? In interviews with potential assistant and principal candidates entering the position, the usual response to the question "Describe the leadership responsibilities that you were given" yields the following common responses from teachers:

- ◆ "I was the grade-level chairperson or department head."
- ◆ "I supervised or coached students in an after school activity or sport."
- ◆ "I helped write a curriculum unit of study."

Experienced assistant principal candidates who describe their previous responsibilities frequently identify skills that are linear and have clear parameters. Skills that require doing tasks as opposed to figuring out how to solve problems are common experiences described by assistant principals: "I supervise the lunchroom, manage traffic duty in the morning and afternoon, supervise custodians and teaching assistants, and handle facilities." When pressed for details concerning the more global experience of running a school, the frequent response is, "I act in the principal's place when they are at meetings or absent from school." As an assistant principal, reflect carefully on what whole-school experiences prepared you to become principal. Whether you are an assistant or a principal, consider this analogy as a way to put the administrative job into perspective.

The Journey Begins

You have been appointed to your new position. You are told that now you get the keys to drive a bus from Miami, Florida, to Seattle, Washington. This is not a trip you have ever taken before but determine that it shouldn't be all that hard because you have received a license to drive the bus, you have watched bus drivers before, you have talked to people who took the trip, and you are a very good driver of your own car. You are ready to go. You count the number of passengers. (How many staff members will be your responsibility? Put that many on your bus.)

When the keys go into the ignition, you begin wondering about the difference between driving the bus and driving your family car. You went to a lot of effort to get your license to drive, but once the passengers got on the bus, it felt different from what you expected. For starters, the bus is a lot bigger, with more seats, more mirrors, and an unusual clutch system. The people on the bus are strangers, and there are a lot of them—all sizes, shapes, and personalities. Everyone expects you to take care of them throughout the trip.

They don't know your plans for the trip, the direction you plan to go, or the length of time you expect the trip to take. But, as the bus driver, it never occurs to you to ask their opinion.

You were given direction from your company to get these people to Seattle as quickly as possible on the shortest possible route. (That makes the trip cost-effective.) No longer can the company afford to have its drivers take any side trips or stop unnecessarily for unplanned excursions. The motto of the company is "No Passenger Left Behind." You have to follow orders. You used to love those times when you could stop, leisurely walk around, and enjoy the uniqueness of the towns and villages. (Oh, for the good old days!) You will take the freeway. You are on your way.

No sooner have you gone down the road than suddenly you start getting different passengers giving you their personal agendas on how to get to Seattle and the directions they want you to take. Several want to go the road most traveled, the safe highway they have always taken on this trip. Others are more adventurous and want to take side roads, drive the long way around, or go to places they have never seen before. Some want to stop frequently to go sightseeing. A few others are willing to go along for the ride. They are the ones who say "Just tell me where you are going, and I'll be fine. Just don't ask me to make any decisions." (Even though the subtext is, "I'll be sure and begin crabbing to my neighbor if the trip isn't going according to my expectations, and you'll be the last to know that I am unhappy.")

Many passengers need more pit stops than you expected, and this becomes irritating. But you deal with it. The first part of the trip is very pleasant. This is easier than you expected given the many war stories that you had heard from other drivers. Already, there are passengers who you want to get to know better, some who are downright cantankerous and annoying, others who are "iffy." Regardless, you plan on a good trip.

Just when you think the trip is going swimmingly and you think everyone recognizes you as a good driver, several things happen that you are totally unprepared for. (1) A terrible rainstorm causes a delay in your plans, causing people to begin fussing that the trip will take too long. (2) Others think you are driving too fast and they don't feel safe. (3) Two passengers start a terrible argument that lasts the entire trip, wearing on everyone's nerves. (4) The dispatcher tells you to take a shorter route than the one you had planned, confusing you and many of your passengers, who begin nagging you to take the original route. (5) You have engine trouble and didn't know how to fix it. (How embarrassing! Your passengers are annoyed that you, a driver, do not know how to repair a bus engine.) This causes another delay while you get help.

You worry that your supervisor will think you are not capable of driving this bus. You will have to push the bus harder and faster to meet the deadline. There are too many interruptions. Cell phones keep ringing when you are trying to concentrate, and four of the travelers simply won't stop talking to you. Two others refuse to talk to you at all.

You get the idea. By the end of the trip you are completely exhausted from the unexpected occurrences, the continuous interruptions, the orders you don't agree with, and the irritating passengers who won't follow your directions. At the end of the trip, you realize that there are five passengers whom you forgot were on the bus. Who are these people? Do they even belong on this bus? You have been a passenger on a bus lots of times, and you think that certainly you didn't act like one of them.

Then, you face the realization that you have to get your passengers back to Miami. You still must drive. How will you get through the trip—again? You wonder why you felt so unprepared for the unknowns. You worry that because you didn't get to Seattle as fast as you had planned, your supervisor from the company will give you "what for." "What if I lose my job?" you wonder. "What could I have done differently? I must regroup, plan a better route, get home faster to make up for lost time. How can I do that?"

When Do I Begin?

From the moment that you are "blessed" by your supervisor, you should begin thinking about how you will approach your new job. Usually, within a week or two you are escorted into the school, where you are introduced to your new staff. However, it could be a few more weeks before you actually move into the school. You need to accomplish every possible task before your assignment begins, and you are bombarded with questions and interruptions as soon as you enter your new school.

What Should I Do and How Should I Do It?

Begin Your Mental Preparation—Now

Review the bus trip metaphor. Were you the driver, manager, leader, or all three? You had a goal that provided you with a clear destination, but along the way, what was lacking? As a manager, you drove the bus, followed your supervisor's rules, and accomplished a task, and you did it well. What was the relationship between the driver and the passengers? At the end of the trip, back in Miami, everyone probably went their own way, and life went on.

Revisit the trip, only this time provide more details and include the positive interaction between the driver and passengers, whereby the driver created a collaborative and democratic environment: a trip on which you and the passengers got to know each other, decided when to stop and take pictures, and chose when to stop and take a walk. You worked together to determine the most effective and exciting way to make the trip an interesting and productive one and still arrive on time.

Imagine the difference in the trip if the passengers could share their previous experiences along the route they had traveled before—if you, the driver, learned from them, and they learned from each other. Not about driving the bus, but how to collaborate and discuss ways to make it the best trip possible. Of course, you would operate within some parameters, but within those guidelines, there would be flexibility to collaboratively make decisions, solve problems, and think of other ways to both enjoy the trip and get the most productivity from the time you have together. That is a good leader. It takes talent in both areas.

The Moment Arrives When You Meet Your New Family

When you are introduced to your new staff, be prepared for an awkward moment. No one really knows what to say. Staff members who do not know you are sizing you up. How do you look? Do you look happy to be there? Are you dressed professionally? Are you nice? Who knows what goes through the hearts and minds of teachers at a time such as this. What went through your mind the first time you were introduced to a new principal?

The most that can be said about these uncomfortable moments is to plan them carefully. The first impression is very important. The staff wants to hear something from you. Write something down so that if you experience "brain freeze" (even veteran principals can get stage fright), you won't feel embarrassed for lack of something to say.

Be brief. Say, for example, "I am honored to be selected to work with you. I am grateful to Supervisor (name) for providing me this opportunity to become part of the (school) community. I look forward to meeting each one of you so that I can find ways to support you and your students. I will be officially on board on (date)." Discuss what your supervisor expects you to do after the introduction.

This experience may range anywhere from leaving quickly to staying around for a more formal reception at which each staff member greets you. Your job is to be pleasant, friendly, and yourself. Smile a lot. It is not a time to make anything other than the most positive comments about the staff, community, and school.

Reflect on the general atmosphere. Don't hang your hat on your first impression. It is too soon to tell.

The time from your official appointment until you actually move into your office will vary from district to district. Usually the turnaround time is quick, sometimes as little as two weeks. Regardless, the mental preparation begins by thinking of a time frame in which you must accomplish large tasks in a short period of time.

Details on how to accomplish each of the following responsibilities are found within the chapters of this book. The steps that follow are designed to get you started. This provides an example of what can be accomplished during the transition time between your appointment and when you receive the keys to your new school.

Prepare a Calendar to Pace Your Time-Sensitive Tasks

This is not the school calendar but one that gives you a sketch of how to pace your year based first on district-level time frames. Regardless of the time frame of your appointment to your new position, the following tasks are consistent with the time frame of most schools. You will make adjustments depending on the specific district's dates for the beginning and ending of the year. This is a basic format to use as an example so that you can see the overall areas that can sneak up on you unless you are careful. You can begin to study this information the moment after your appointment, even before you officially get the keys. This is working fast and efficient

Pay particular attention to the number of days during November and December. Vacation time during those two months can really eat up instructional days. Also note the number of days available before standardized testing occurs. Chapter 8 provides additional details on analyzing instructional time.

Hang on to this calendar for now. Chapter 2 describes a meeting with your predecessor and key staff members who will work during the summer, such as your secretary, assistant (if you have one), or guidance counselor. Take this with you and ask him or her to add to it.

The following list is not intended to detail all of the many things that you need to accomplish during each month. Rather, this is an example, a start that you will complete as you look at the specific school needs and practices. Time adjustments will vary depending on the beginning and ending dates of the school year. Items identified below are described in detail throughout this book.

Checklist of Items to Add to the Yearly Calendar

Two months before school begins

- ◆ Complete the hiring process. Determine whether there are any unfilled vacancies. If so, identify an interviewing process.
- ◆ Begin analyzing testing data (last two years).
- ◆ Meet with small groups of key people.
- ◆ Develop an organizational system to keep track of management tasks.
- ◆ Carefully study the union contract; it could affect staff schedules.
- ◆ Pay particular attention to the details of staff members' assessments. Read them all.
- ◆ Send your letter of introduction and call each staff member to introduce yourself.
- ◆ Meet with the person in charge of the master schedule. Receive an explanation about the rationale behind the schedule.
- ◆ Study the school yearbook; familiarize yourself with every faculty member so that when you meet him or her, you will already have connected a name with a face.

One or two months before school begins

- ◆ Complete a planning schedule for teachers before the opening of school, including a focused event (Alvy and Robbins, 1998).
- ◆ Convene the Leadership Team.

- Meet with small groups of key people to learn about the existing School Improvement Plan.
- Discuss any immediate interventions that must occur to meet student needs regarding standardized testing.
- Provide a questionnaire for teachers to read before your meetings with them in September.
- Meet with parent groups (PTA, PTO, and School Advisory Council).
- Arrange with the parent organization to add your signature to the bank signature verification form.
- Develop a plan to ensure that every student in the school knows who you are and what you look like.

First month of school

- Complete your meetings with each staff member.
- Establish a system for scheduling formal observations.
- Establish a schedule to ensure that blocks of time are set aside every day for drop-in visits to each staff member's workplace: classrooms, lunchroom, music, art, coach, custodian, teaching assistants, everyone.

Second month of school

- Depending on the size of the school, the first formal observations may need to begin, including post-observation conferences.
- Identify and organize meetings with key leaders in each grade level, department, or support staff to help you begin to learn and understand unfamiliar curriculum.

Third month of school

- Begin to determine how you will approach the implementation of your vision for the upcoming year.
- Complete the first round of formal observations and conferences.

Fourth month of school/end of first semester

- Begin identifying the number of students for next year.
- Begin the preliminary stages of your budget for next year.

Fifth month of school

- Meet with the necessary groups to begin formulating your School Improvement Plan for next year.

- Determine the testing procedures and coordinate procedural tasks with the responsible members of the staff. (Make sure you know how the logistics of this entire process works and who is in charge.)
- Identify the accountability issues concerning testing protocol and the security issues surrounding the testing.

Sixth month of school

- Begin the final round of assessments (check again the time frames with your district and the contract language).
- If there is someone who may need termination at the end of the year, make sure you are in contact with your supervisor and anyone at the county level responsible for helping you with that decision.

Seventh month of school

- Complete the final observations and conferences.
- Begin completing your end-of-the-year assessments and conferences.
- If you will house a summer school, begin making plans for the details for this program.
- Complete your budget and meet with your supervisor to seek advice and to clarify if you are "doing it right."
- Prepare for the standardized testing frenzy.

Eighth month of school

- Informal observations continue.
- Begin planning staff development for next year. Meet with your Leadership Team and any other committees to make sure your vision and the vision of the school are compatible.
- Now you can begin taking small steps toward moving the school forward. What are those steps going to look like?
- Send out letters of intent to each teacher so that you can determine which staff members would like to return to the school next year.
- If there are teachers you will dismiss, make sure you are in contact with the district's people, who will walk you through the final stages of the process. Watch the union contract dates.

Ninth month of school

- You've almost made it. Keep going—you will get there.
- Finalize the budget and the numbers you need to staff the school next year.

◆ Complete plans for summer school.

End of the school year

 ◆ By now, your testing data should be back in your hands.

 ◆ This year you had to analyze the data in a short period of time.

 ◆ Based on the scores, staffing may change. Study these data before making the final decision about which staff will be assigned where.

Summer break

 ◆ You start all over again. Reflect on last year. What did you learn?

 ◆ What will you do in a different and better way this coming school year?

 ◆ How will you make a greater impact in the realization of your vision?

 ◆ Clean out your files and reorganize important information.

Questions and Answers

Q: Why should I start getting tasks and timelines organized before I even get into the school?

A: The purpose of organizing important time lines is based on the need to accomplish tasks as soon as possible. Any task you can accomplish before you get into the school is one fewer task you will have to crowd into a busy schedule once you begin.

Also, schools operate on a calendar year, not a school year. As a result, tasks that require large amounts of time can sneak up on you. If you are not careful, you will find yourself scrambling at the last minute to meet important deadlines that you easily could have arranged early because the timelines are based on union contracts or district requirements.

For example, classroom assessments are an important part of your job. What if you let the time slip by, and you didn't even get into all of the classrooms several times before formal assessments are due? Suddenly, you have to marathon your assessments. This is not the way to become a successful evaluator of staff. Chapter 7 elaborates ways to accomplish effective assessments.

Timelines are critical. Your method and the specifics about that organization will become yours. You will find the one that meets your needs. Find it quickly. More about organizational strategies can be found in Chapter 5.

Q: I don't think my background experiences will influence my leadership. Why is it important to factor that in?

A: Some examples may help:

You were undoubtedly a successful teacher, and you knew what it took to become one; will that influence you in your assessment of a less-than-capable teacher?

You were probably a successful student, learning in a specific way; will that influence what you expect curriculum and instructional strategies to look like?

If you are a working parent who arranges for emergency day care, how will you react to a teacher who consistently takes time off from work when his or her children are sick?

You always dress professionally, how will you react if some of your staff members dress inappropriately?

It is important to acknowledge and reflect on your decisions when your own experiences influence ways you respond. Thinking about these issues before you actually are faced with them will prevent reaction and provide action behaviors that could keep you from getting into trouble.

True Story

> I had a new teacher who thought she was a size 2, when she was really a size 14, and she thought she looked just fine. Where was her mother? I must have talked to her three or four times about her dress, and she just didn't get it. Then I began wondering, if she won't respond to my request that she dress professionally, what else won't she do?
>
> —Middle School assistant principal

Q: What if there are staff positions that need filling, but I have no idea what type of person I need for the school?

A: Coordinate a schedule so that members of the department or team can interview with you. Agree ahead of time about what characteristics constitute the best qualifications and which person could best fit the philosophy of the school and the personalities of the other team members. You don't know the teams well enough to hire without the help of others.

Survival Tips

- *Take advantage of every moment to think about "what if ..." based on the issues that are important to you.* You won't act on anything but the most glaring issues during the first two months. But if you have a notion of how you would react, it saves time and energy.

- *Spend time before your assignment begins on the nuts and bolts of getting the year started (assuming you were appointed in the summer).* You can waste a lot of time up front worrying about things you will have no control over. Concentrate on the issues that will become your immediate responsibility and that you can sink your teeth into.

- *Work methodically through the suggestions in this book to help you focus.* Pay particular attention to how quickly the year goes.

- *Recognize your own issues, accept them, and determine modifications you will need in your own behavior* to make the principal or assistant principal experience a positive one in your new environment.

- *Begin thinking of things that "push your buttons."* Before your assignment begins, it is helpful to think of things you find you cannot live with, even if you are new to a school. Some practices that you see when you examine the culture are things you must do something about. Look around your existing environment (the school where you currently work). Are there practices occurring in your current school that, as a principal, you could not "look the other way"? How is the current principal handling those issues? Is that what you would do?

The following examples may appear trivial, but unfortunately, the simplest things can become huge problems unless you are prepared and handle them carefully. What other things would you add to the list? Which things don't bother you?

- Teachers who correct papers during your staff meetings.
- Staff members who are consistently late for your meetings, appointments, or dismissal of students from class.
- Staff members who consistently leave campus the second that their contracted day is over—or sooner—even if it means leaving an important meeting.

- Chewing gum, keeping a soda on the desk, munching on snacks while teaching.
- Answering cell phone calls during class instruction.
- Consistently turning in required paperwork late.
- Taking every day off that their contract allows (and there is nothing you can do about it).
- Dressing unprofessionally.

It All Depends on the Hill You Want to Die On

For the sake of your sanity, assume that in your entire administrative career, you are allowed only one hill to die on. This is much more important than the traditional adage to "choose your battles." This is a once-in-a-lifetime decision that could help you to distinguish the important from the unimportant issues on which you will stand firm. A button that is pushed may not be *the* hill, but simply a button.

Choose it carefully, choose it well, and choose it one time, forever.

Summary

As a new principal or assistant principal, you must work *smart*, *fast*, and *efficient*. You made a big decision, usually involving many people, before you decided to enter the world of school administration. You chose to leave behind the security of your teaching position.

As a teacher, you controlled your environment. As an assistant, you worked with fairly tight job parameters. You have your own inner purpose, a background of experiences, and your own vision that will drive your leadership strategies. Ten key factors are identified at the end of this chapter as important areas for the principal to keep in mind when moving along the continuum of understanding the job.

As the new principal, when you enter a school where everything is your personal responsibility, it doesn't take much to feel overwhelmed. The job just doesn't feel like you thought it would.

The metaphor used in this chapter described the conditions under which a principal feels prepared for the assignment. Then, he or she quickly realizes that the complexities of personalities, directions from supervisors, time restraints, and unexpected happenings can alter plans in the blink of an eye. The distinction between manager and leader remains a critical understanding on your journey into the principal's world. The tour bus story resembles the school environment. An effective trip requires both an effective manager and leader.

Principals and assistants must use time wisely. Between the time of appointment to the position and receiving the keys to the kingdom, it is possible to begin several tasks identified in this chapter.

- Reexamine your purpose, motivation and driving forces—who are you?
- Identify the broad-range view of the year beginning with district timelines. This occurs in list form and by the month to give you a sense of the importance of time management.
- Identify issues and concerns that push your buttons. This involves discovering the immediate needs of the school and issues that you absolutely can't live with for any length of time.

Time is easily wasted when you don't know how to determine what is important and what can wait until later. It is difficult to understand how to organize and prioritize the issues when so many things come at you at once. If you have a clear understanding of the important tasks and skills you need to accomplish and when you need to accomplish them, then all the crazy things that come your way won't blindside you.

Reflections

1. Describe your inner purpose. How do you think your inner purpose will determine how you will lead the school? What words can you use that define who you are in relation to your job? What words define you as a manager compared to those that define you as a leader? Once the words are in place, write a statement that describes your sense of purpose as a manager and a leader.

2. Discuss the metaphor of the tour bus trip, you as the driver, and each of the complexities of the job that occurred in the story. What did the scenario describe?

   What behaviors differentiated the driver as manager or the driver as leader? Explain your answer.

3. Think about issues in your existing school that, if you were principal, you would not tolerate or would change immediately. How would you make immediate changes and not antagonize the current faculty?

4. Explain why it is important to complete as many basic management tasks as quickly as possible, even before you actually receive the keys to the school. What advantages are there in planning the entire year

based on the district-level requirements before receiving the schedule of individual school events? What information could you get at your existing school that would help you begin developing your schedule?

5. Although the potential "to do" list for the year appears in this chapter, it is intended to give you a quick overview of what to expect, and it is not comprehensive. You will create an extensive list as you go through the year. Create a list of tasks that you can accomplish before you actually move into your office. In the calendar you develop, identify and schedule your first four weeks after your appointment to the position. Describe why you selected the tasks and how you intend to accomplish them.

2

Building Background: Separating the Forest from the Trees

(Two Months before the Teachers Arrive)

You have received the keys to the kingdom, your new school, and as principal, it is all yours. As an assistant principal, you may have a new boss, or this may be a new school for you also.

You have examined your core beliefs. You began a calendar to get a general idea of the time frame of district requirements, particularly for the first month after your appointment. You thought about those things that would bother you the most if you saw them in your new school. You may even think of ways to handle them. But there is a lot more to do and not much time.

Schools have a history, and it is your responsibility to understand that history as quickly as possible. Granted, you will begin your own history, but it won't happen for another year or two at least.

Your next step requires studying and understanding how the school has evolved. This examination will give you the background knowledge about the school that you will need in each subsequent endeavor.

Now you begin talking to yourself. Even scarier, you will start answering yourself. That's OK—it's an occupational hazard. You have a lot to learn and analyze. You have to talk to someone, why not yourself? Sooner than it seems possible, you will see your new staff. Next time, it will be more than an introduction. They will be yours. You must work *smart*, *fast*, and *efficient*.

When Do I Begin?

Two months before the teachers arrive. You have from now until the teachers start coming, if you were hired during the summer. Get going. Before the first official staff meeting, you are on a fact-finding mission, nothing more. It becomes counterproductive to spend huge amounts of time drawing conclusions on your own.

In-depth conclusions will occur after meeting with the groups identified throughout this chapter and as you progress through the year. The guided questions provided here may save you time as you interview key members of the school community.

What Should I Do and How Should I Do It?

Analyze the Facts

Before the teaching staff arrives for the start of the school year, familiarize yourself with all the information available regarding your new school. This will provide you with "questions I ask myself," "questions I ask others," and "food for thought." Methodically studying everything you can will help you to avoid saying and doing things you may regret later. Foot-in-mouth disease is one nasty bug.

This is the time to read school documents, take notes, clarify the information, and study your findings. Specific details will follow in this chapter.

To efficiently study the hard data, you must work when and where you won't be interrupted. This becomes off-the-clock (when you will not be interrupted) focus and study time. This is no time to try to delegate any task or discuss this with anyone. You need personal *think time*.

Figure out a System to Keep Track of your Findings

You will soon meet with staff members and gather a lot of information. Plan ahead for the fastest and most efficient way to record your findings. Will you use file folders, the computer, the latest handheld technology, cell phone, sticky notes, or hand-written notes?

At the beginning of the fact-finding mission, it will be easy to remember everything. This lasts about three days, when suddenly the information begins to blur. You know it will only get worse. Without a system for keeping track of conversations and paper, you will get consumed by some "memory-eating" virus before you even begin. (For more on the organizational part of the job, see Chapter 5.)

One list is divided into three sections that organize one round of information:

1. Questions I ask myself: "I don't get it. Why not?"
2. Questions I ask others: "Help me understand…"
3. Food for thought: "This doesn't seem to fit my beliefs—why not?"

How Did the School Evolve?
Learn the School History

Study every written document you can find about the school for at least the last two years. Usually the secretary can provide you with this information. If no one knows where anything is, you have another question to add to your list.

Assume there are documents to read. If you do not understand what you read, chances are nobody else can either. Make another note. Someone may have overlooked information that needs clarification. Place this under your *Questions to Ask Others*. Review this later with someone who can help you understand what on earth is going on.

If procedures and policies are unclear, ask why. Possibilities include the following:

- ◆ If your predecessor was at the school for a long time, chances are there are many unwritten practices and old information.
- ◆ If the majority of the staff has been at the school for quite a while, it may be that no one felt a need to update policies that were understood, not written. Were teachers new to the school on their own to figure out school policies?
- ◆ If your predecessor was there less than three years, the written policies and practices may be disconnected, confusing, and in need of revision.

Study the history of the school through scrapbooks, yearbooks, the school web site, or any other written information that provides an understanding of how the school has evolved. This will reveal things the school and community value. Make a note of the areas that have received the most publicity. Ask yourself, why did the school showcase this? Perhaps there is no recent pictorial representation that chronicles the history and events of the school, not even videotapes of events. If not, why? If so, look them over at home when you can. (So much for watching the game on television; tell yourself you are studying your own game tapes.)

True Story

> The first thing I told my new secretary was "Let's take down that portrait of my predecessor, he looks like he is scaring everyone to death." It was then that I learned he walked by the school every day to see if it was still there. He is still an influential deacon in the community church. Thank goodness she said something. I almost blew it my first week on the job." (He is still there, looming down, and he still looks scary.)
>
> —Elementary school principal

Study the School Web Site (If There Is One)

This is another way to determine the image that the school portrays to the school community. This will help as you continue to understand the culture. What messages are confusing or unclear to you? Who is in charge of the web site, including links, downloadable documents, and internet access?

Read and Study Documents on Curriculum, Instruction, and Assessment

What information is available about each area of the curriculum? Draw conclusions by studying the available written curriculum and instruction documents.

Curriculum

- ◆ If you can't find explanations about each area of the curriculum, why not?
- ◆ Do you find only documents that are generated as state or national benchmarks or standards, but no explanation of how teachers implement them at your new school? Perhaps you find some curricular areas, but not all.
- ◆ How were the decisions made regarding curriculum (what is taught), instruction (how it is taught), and assessment (how do you know students learned?) You may need to add this to your Questions to Ask Others list.

- Make another note about areas of the curriculum about which you have no clue. Be honest with yourself. If you have no experience or frame of reference in any area of the curriculum, admit it, note it, and think about how you will learn more about those subject or support areas.

Instruction

What topics and concepts are taught in each instructional area? Why?

☐ Teacher always taught the topic and concepts with no other criteria.

☐ Standardized tests drive the topics and concepts.

☐ The basic textbooks drive the topics and concepts.

☐ State standards and benchmarks drive the topics and concepts.

☐ The grade level, team, or department determined it is necessary because students need it when they take the next course in the sequence.

☐ What are your personal beliefs on this subject?

What Do You Really Understand about Curriculum, Instruction, and Assessment in Every Instructional Area in the School?

You have examined the hard data from standardized testing by teacher, department, or grade level and can see where the holes are or your confusion occurs. You will make lots of notes in areas in which you are unclear about informal and authentic classroom assessments. (You will get more clarification when you meet with teams.)

- List each department, grade level, or team.
- Put a code by each subject area, support position, or program, such as media, guidance, exceptional education, English as a second language learners, and specialized programs or classrooms that you need to understand better. Code the areas about which you have no clue. Make a special note to concentrate on learning more about those areas.

  Hint: The most common areas in which principals lack direct experience are exceptional education and English as a second language programs. Perhaps your new school has other categorical money to support additional projects or programs. (Government subsidized programs are heavily monitored. You must learn all areas, and learn them well.)

Your experiences as a high school student and in your college programs may have provided you with some understanding of extracurricular activities beyond specific content. This knowledge is limited to your personal participation. Perhaps you sang in the chorus or played in the band; maybe you were a debater, skier, swimmer, golfer, or technology nerd—whatever. It is natural that you will be more familiar with some areas than others: Recognize it and note it.

How will you learn all the complex areas that are not in your comfort zone? You will get in the trenches with every staff member.

The word spreads like wildfire. Teachers will quickly let others on the staff know that you were interested enough in an unfamiliar area to spend time with them. Learn from them, then pay similar attention to everyone else.

Assessment

- Where do you go to find out the types of student assessments used?
- Does it seem as if standardized testing is the primary assessment used to make instructional decisions? What else is used? How often?
- What is the difference among and between individual teachers' methods of assessment?
- If you can not figure it out, find out why the individual methods of assessment are not clear.
- What expectations for student performance are reflected in the assessments used? How do you know? Is the documentation complete?
- Can you determine whether assessment is driving instruction?
- You have no idea what assessments look like in certain classrooms. List those classrooms. You will need this information when you observe teachers.
- What are your personal beliefs about assessment?
- What is the expectation for teacher assessments and required documentation at the district level?
- What are your supervisor's expectations?

Scrutinize the Standardized Test Scores

Analyzing test scores is a complex process. You will examine the assessment documents and draw your own conclusions before meeting with others. You can discuss your assumptions and ask questions of others based on the facts. The staff will be so impressed when you can cite numbers and school test data, they will think you are so on top of things (one might hope).

Compare this year's scores with last year's state, national, and possibly local standardized test scores according to the following categories:

- Total scores by grade, by department level, and by teacher
- Total scores by subgroups
  - Minority groups individually and compared to each other
  - Special needs students
  - Boys and girls
- Mobility and its effect on scores
- Students on free and reduced lunches and the effect on scores and subgroups.
- Rate of student improvement in individual groups, such as minority and second-language learners, among and between grade levels, and individual improvement within each classroom.
- Rate of student improvement among low-performing students
- Rate of student improvement among high-performing students

Compare each set of data from one year to the next. Create your own document or system so that you have the numbers and conclusions at your fingertips.

By What Criteria Are Students Placed in Classes?

- If you can't figure it out, you need to find out why policies and practices are not clear.
- Is the placement of students in classrooms clearly defined?
- How did your predecessor do this? You need to learn from this.
- What are the criteria for placing students in classrooms?
- Are students placed in classrooms based upon test scores? If so, which tests are used? List them.
- Who makes the decisions on student placement?
- Who is in charge of the master schedule?
- What do you believe about the school's practice? (Keep it to yourself for now.)
- What percentage of the students in the school are assigned to special programs such as exceptional education, second-language learners, International Baccalaureate, or gifted?

Clarify Other Topics Relating to Curriculum, Instruction, and Assessment that Come to Your Attention

- ◆ Is there a schoolwide grading policy? If so, what is the practice?
- ◆ What is the school's homework policy? Do individual departments agree on a homework policy? Do you agree with it?

Analyze the Demographics.

- ◆ Where do the students go when they transfer?
  - To schools in the same vicinity?
  - Do they just move from one project or apartment complex to the other, rotating among the same cluster of schools?
  - Do they move to a different town, state, or country?
  - When students withdraw, how many return to the school within the same year?
  - Do families seem to pull their children out of school with little warning? (If you don't know, add this to your Questions to Ask Others list).
- ◆ What are the demographics surrounding the school?
  - Socioeconomic levels
  - Numbers on free and reduced lunches by class or grade level
  - Number of buses that transport students
  - Type of housing: apartments, homeless shelters, single-family homes, upscale houses, farms, or trailers.
- ◆ Typically, where do the students go after school?
  - Latchkey children
  - After-school care sponsored by the school
  - Private day care
  - Private sports centers: YMCA, Boys' and Girls' Clubs
  - Care of an older sibling
  - Full- or part-time job

If you can't find the answer in the documents, continue adding this to your Questions to Ask Others list.

Compile basic information about the individual teachers; list or create a form to keep track of your findings. When you contact each teacher (described in Chapter 3), you can add these facts to your inquiries. This is the first task you can actually assign to someone else. If your secretary is not available, guess what? You do it yourself. Collect the following information about each teacher:

- ◆ Teacher's name
- ◆ Years of total teaching experience
- ◆ Number of years at this school
- ◆ Academic degree
- ◆ Area of certification
- ◆ Teaching assignment
- ◆ Length of time teaching in this assignment
- ◆ Race
- ◆ Gender
- ◆ Received or working on National Board Certification

In addition, collect information about the group of teachers:

- ◆ Number of teachers with fewer than three years of experience
- ◆ Number of teachers with more than 15 years of experience

This is a lot of information to digest. How does this information affect your understanding of the culture? Your primary responsibility begins by asking the hard questions. Why do they do it this way? Or, this doesn't make sense—why? This is a tedious, methodical, and *smart* way to thoughtfully understand the facts about your staff.

Questions to Ask Yourself

Analyze Your Personal Background of Experiences to Begin Formulating Your Own Personal Beliefs

This is something you can do coming and going from school, in the shower, fixing dinner, from two to four in the morning, whenever. It is important to begin thinking about your own educational experiences before you draw objective conclusions from the data gathered. Your background could affect your belief system and your expectations for the staff and students—but should it?

- ◆ How did you learn during most of your educational experiences at each level: elementary, high school, undergraduate, and educational leadership classes?
  - • You were told what to do, and you did it.
  - • You learned what you were told to learn.

- You were a curious learner.
- You wanted to learn everything you could.
- You thought a lot about what you learned.
- You understood what you experienced because you received a lot of opportunities to explore ideas and draw your own conclusions.
- You created a lot of projects that helped you understand the concept being taught.
- You created a lot of projects that didn't teach you a thing.

◆ What is your learning and leadership style?
  - You are very reflective, and you think continuously about how you can learn more.
  - You like to cut to the chase because you know what you need to do, and you do it.
  - You are most comfortable when you tell people what to do, and you expect them to do it because you are the principal or assistant principal.
  - You want to make sure that you are doing the right thing. You like a lot of collaboration when you're learning something. You want to make sure you are doing it the right way.
  - You like getting people together over coffee to visit and discuss solutions to problems.

◆ What was your teaching style?
  - You knew your subject well. You taught using the required book.
  - You used some videos with your students and primarily used the required book.
  - Your classes received a lot of higher-level questioning from you.
  - You didn't actually have a typical classroom: Your background was in physical education, guidance, media specialist, or any other non-classroom-based position.
  - You worked mostly by yourself, and you preferred that.
  - You liked working with the colleagues from whom you learned, brainstorming ideas while trying to figure out better instructional strategies.

◆ What is your management style?
  - How will your own background influence your expectations of others?

- Will you use all leadership styles depending on the circumstances?
- Will you assume that what the staff sees is what they get?
- How will you learn to adjust your leadership and learning style to the situation?
- Will this be possible if you are comfortable with your style and assume everyone else will just have to live with it?
- Will you carefully choose your words and learn to think carefully about what you want to accomplish before you say and do anything?

As you think about the statements and questions above, you really do begin talking to yourself. That is OK, it just gets worse—principals and assistants also answer themselves. This just made you your own best friend. You have left your teachers' support groups behind.

True Story

I'll never forget my first Friday after school opened. I overheard the teachers planning to get together after work. They left and I stared at the papers piled in front of me. It sure was a different feeling.

—High school principal

Questions to Ask Others

Meet with Key External Support Persons (Those Who Work Outside Campus)

During the second phase of understanding the journey, you are no longer alone. You will now combine what you discovered with what others might know. These are the support people who have traveled this route before and serve as guides.

You have analyzed the data and listed questions to ask yourself and others. It is time to connect your notes with the perceptions you gathered. Now you will put them together with others who may help you to put other pieces of the puzzle together.

Meet with Your Supervisor

As soon as you analyze all of the data and clean up your notes so that you are well organized, arrange a meeting with your supervisor. Take your data. Prepare an agenda to cover each of the areas in which you have questions. Take notes from your supervisor's responses.

Your goals are the following:

- Learn how much you can count on your supervisor for support.
- Let your supervisor know that you need his or her advice to make sure you do the right things in your school.
- Begin forming a bond (you need your supervisor—a lot).
- Do not try to appear overconfident. There is a very fine line between portraying your capabilities for the job and arrogance. Below are some questions that can guide you through the discussion and demonstrate your motivation to learn the job.

True Story

> I always worry that my boss will think I'm not able to do my job if I ask a lot of questions.
>
> —Middle school principal

The following are guiding questions for your meeting with your supervisor:

- What is your perception of the school as a whole?
- Describe the areas within the school that you believe I should concentrate on.
- I know I am new to the school and I have a lot to learn. As the new kid on the block, will you view me as less competent if I ask a lot of questions?
- What is the chain of command if I run into a problem at school? For example, I might find that we are very short of substitutes, yet the central office is taking forever to process applications for those positions. Do I call the head of substitutes to complain, or do you want me to call you first?
- I have a crabby parent. At what point in the process of handling this person do you want to be informed?

- What is the relationship between school board members and principals and teachers? In other words, what should I do if an individual school board member calls me and wants to visit the school? What should I do if I am asked a question I'm not comfortable answering?

- I will do everything I can to stay out of trouble. Can you anticipate issues that could happen at the school and tell me what things I should be careful about?

- Will you explain the budget to me in terms of rationale for various line items? Or, would you recommend someone I can go to so that I can thoroughly understand this school's budget?

- What concerns do you have about the amount of money available for the school?

- What other sources of funding are available to the school?

- What is the relationship of the school to the business community?

- How much effort do you recommend I put into soliciting local business support for the school? How important is that to you as my supervisor?

- Could you recommend someone I can go to so that I don't always have to ask you so many questions?

- Do you think my predecessor would make a good mentor? Do you serve that role?

- What advice can you give me?

True Story

> If he had just come to me first, I would have walked him through what to do. He tried to handle this on his own and now we have a mess to fix.
>
> —Supervisor regarding a principal

Meet with Your Predecessor

Another lunch is in order. (Realize that this lunch thing only happens before the school year begins. Take advantage of it while you can.) Take a very sharp pencil; you have a lot to learn from this person. Ask him or her to bring the calendars from last year on which district timelines are identified. Bring your calendar. In this way, you can compare schedules and events. Also bring the school yearbook to reference individual teachers.

For this meeting, whether your predecessor will become your mentor does not matter. There are very specific things that only your predecessor knows. You need that information. Arrange to meet as soon as possible after your appointment to the position. This should occur before you get the keys to the school. It's working faster and more efficiently.

Your predecessor certainly has more history than you do with the school. You need to know what he or she experienced. Organize your notes and focus on things you have read and studied that you didn't understand at all or that you need to know more details concerning how issues developed and how problems were solved.

When you spend time with your predecessor asking questions from your own findings, you will get a sense of his or her administrative style. Your predecessor's style may help you to understand why and how teachers respond to your decisions or comments.

The following are guiding questions for your meeting with your predecessor:

- What issues have haunted the school forever? You might have an example similar to this one: "The first thing I heard from parents I talked to, 'Why don't you get that traffic light put in on the corner?' Come to find out, the highway wouldn't put a light there in spite of ten years worth of parent lobbying."
- How long were you at the school?
- Why did you leave?
- If you had remained at the school, what would your priorities include?
- What are the greatest strengths in the school?
- What are the greatest challenges in the school?
- How have the demographics of the community changed in the last five years?
- Were you planning to dismiss any staff member this year? Who? Why?
- Where is the documentation that I can use to continue the process?
- If there is a dismissal planned, whom do I contact to work with me as the process continues?
- Are there any staff members who gave you a particular amount of grief?
- Who were they, and what were the circumstances?
- Who were the curriculum leaders in the school?

- Describe the exceptional education and English as a second language programs in the school.
- What was your belief about issues of inclusion at the school?
- Whom did you count on as the school cheerleaders?
- What is the school's claim to fame?
- Talk to me about the staff in the front office, including their strengths and concerns.
- In whom can I confide and know they will not break a confidence?
- What would cause me to get into trouble?
- How much support can I expect from my supervisor?
- When and with which groups was the most recent audit of the books conducted?
- Where can I find the details about how money is collected, accounted for, and deposited at events where cash and checks are given?
- Did you select any specific program for low-performing students?
- Who is in charge of identifying such programs? Is the decision made by the individuals or teams affected by the selection?
- What process is used when making curriculum decisions?
- What role did you assume in issues regarding curriculum, instruction, and assessments?
- Who is in charge of fixed assets? What is the status of that accountability?

If you have one or more assistant principals, ask the following questions:

- What specific tasks were assigned to each assistant?
- Would you change their tasks for the coming year?
- What is the level of competence of each assistant?
- How long do you see the assistant staying in his or her position?
- What are each assistant's strengths and weaknesses?
- Overall, what advice can you give me?

If you conclude that your predecessor would be a good mentor, ask for help and make sure you can keep in contact.

Meet with Your Assistant or Assistants (If You Have One or More)

Meet with each assistant as soon as possible. The information you learn from your predecessor will provide further direction in terms of your conversation.

The following are guiding questions for your meeting with your assistant:

- How long have you been in this position at this school?
- What jobs have you been assigned?
- Are these jobs the same ones you want to continue for this coming year? Why or why not?
- What are your career goals?
- Where do you see yourself in two years?
- What are your strengths? Are you utilizing those strengths in your current assignments?
- What are your specific talents and interests? Are those talents and interests utilized at the school? Could they be used? How?
- In what areas do you face the greatest challenges? Why?
- Describe a typical day (if there is such a thing).
- In your perfect world, would you change anything about this school? What? Why?
- What things would you not change? Why?
- Are there any staff members we need to worry about? Who are they?
- What is the problem? What were the plans to help them?
- What are your responsibilities for assessing staff members' performance?
- Who have you been assigned to evaluate?
- Review each of the staff member's assessments for which you are responsible. In this way, you can bring me up to speed on each teacher's level of competence.
- What role do you play in curriculum, instruction, and assessment? How have you proceeded to learn curricula that are outside your area of expertise?
- In what specific ways do you keep the principal informed of your school responsibilities with students, with staff members, with parents, and with community groups?

True Story

My assistant had been at the school for a couple of years before I was hired. At first it seemed that all the teachers kept going to her for everything. I felt 'out of the loop' a lot. My assistant seemed to like the power, and whenever she had a chance it seemed she was undermining me. We had a long talk about my expectations and ways we could support each other. She agreed. I realized the importance of frequent and scheduled meetings with her to clarify our roles. I made a major commitment to keep those times to talk.

—Middle school principal

Meet with Your Administrative Secretary

Assuming the administrative secretary was employed at the school before you came, arrange a meeting. This is the person who knows the school from a very important and interesting perspective. You may begin by asking questions, practicing active listening, and asking for help. In this way, you can learn the dynamics of the office staff from the secretary's point of view. Take lots of notes and study them. Don't forget the food.

Your secretary is so important this deserves a lunch. It's the least you can do to begin building trust between you.

The following are guiding questions for your meeting with your administrative secretary:

- How long have you been in this position at this school?
- What jobs have you been assigned?
- Who asks you to perform other tasks or jobs besides the principal? What are those other jobs?
- If there is a need to contact someone to fix a maintenance problem that the custodian can't, who usually does that? What is the procedure for making that contact?
- Explain how fire drills are conducted. Who keeps track of them?
- Explain who keeps track of internal accounts. How is the money generated that goes into those accounts?
- Explain the staff turnover rate over the last two years.
- Can you think of any explanation for the turnover? If there is no turnover, why?
- Help me understand the office staff operations. Are you considered the office manager as well?
- Describe the role that each office staff member plays.

- Do you feel that the office staff is a cohesive team? If not, why not?
- I am going to meet with others on the office staff. What can I expect may be the concerns that they share?
- Is there anyone who also knows your job?
- Who in the office is cross-trained and in which jobs?
- How are office jobs covered in someone's absence?
- Is anyone else trained to fill in for your position when you are absent?
- What advice would you give me about working at this school?

Meet with the Bookkeeper

Depending on the size of the school, another office staff member may hold the bookkeeper position. Although an annual audit report is part of the general procedures at the school, as the new principal, it is important to request an audit of the books immediately. Also request last year's audit report and have the bookkeeper describe the process used.

As principal, you may be responsible for the entire general budgeting process. In larger districts, a central office department provides the budget to you, and you work within their parameters. Regardless of the procedures, you have to know the budgeting process and procedures from one end to the other. Although your educational leadership classes gave you a basic background for school finance, each school has individual situations you must understand. Request a Bookkeeping 101 lesson from the bookkeeper at your school. Learn the internal accounting procedures expected at the district level. Get additional training from the district-level god or goddess of school budgets. You want to know and learn from this person.

The following are guiding questions for your meeting with the bookkeeper:

- Explain the auditing procedures and review the last audit report with me.
- What are the biggest concerns that you have relating to issues of internal accounts and auditing at the school?
- Explain all of the accounts and procedures for which you are responsible.
- Where can I find the details about how money is collected, accounted for, and deposited at events or for other purposes where cash and checks are given to someone other than you?
- If you are absent for any length of time, is anyone in the office cross-trained to do your job?

True Story

I carefully examine the accounting sheets the bookkeeper gave me every month to sign. Everything seemed in order. I had no idea that she was forging my name to bank deposits. At the end of the year, the auditor found thousands of dollars missing from the school account that went back several years. My predecessor didn't catch it either. It took forever to get it straightened out and ate huge amounts of my time. The bookkeeper was indicted, and I was not held responsible, but I kept asking myself how I could have prevented this from happening.

—Elementary school principal

Meet with Other Groups: Custodians, Office Staff, Food Service Staff, Crossing Guards, Bus Drivers (If They Are Available), and Security Staff

For efficiency's sake, set aside one full day and meet with one group after the other in 45 minute blocks. This will save time because you can set up a continental breakfast for the morning groups; sandwich fixings for the lunch groups; and cookies and beverages for the afternoon groups.

Send out an invitation to each member of the group to set the stage for a get-together. This is a good time to invite any new members of the group to meet their colleagues.

The goal is to let each person know that you value them and want to work closely with them. Trust building begins now. Listen to the direct and implied perceptions of each of the support staff members, defined here as any group of employees who serve the school. Those who are not considered teachers often feel the most overlooked and undervalued. Treat noninstructional staff with equal dignity and respect. Personal attention and acknowledgement of each member's important contribution to the school provides ownership in helping to make the school a place where everyone can be proud.

On the other hand, whether or not you solicit their concerns and issues, you'll probably hear them anyway. Be prepared. You'll probably hear about every issue that was left unresolved, based on the perceptions of the members, and about what your predecessor may or may not have done, both real and imagined. The expectation will be that you will fix every problem yesterday. Acknowledge everything, promise nothing, but state that you will examine the information and look into it.

Remember, never criticize your predecessor. If someone complains, "Our old principal never took care of this or that," say, "My job is to help you do the best possible job. We're in this together. As soon as I find out all the details I will let you know what I found out." (Don't forget to do what you say.)

This is not the time to issue decrees about your expectations; rather, this is the time to informally get to know the people who will be supporting you. Find out about their families, what they like to do outside school, and what their current job involves. This is the time to let the groups learn more about you.

Observe the personal interactions among the group. How do they naturally interact with you? Your observations will come in handy later on, when your meetings are directed to specific issues and solving problems together. Take note of the following:

- What kind of interactions occur among the groups?
- Are they comfortable with each other and seem to like each other?
- Is there anyone who seems removed from the group as a whole?
- Are they friendly to you?
- Are they reluctant to talk to you? (This may imply issues from their past experiences; make a mental note that this lack of interaction requires investigation. Ask the hard question: Did a breakdown in trust occur? How? Why?)

Continued Interaction and Support

The first informal get-together is important. You can start putting names with faces and faces with the jobs that people do in the school. Of course, that is not enough. The next phase of your interaction requires that you go to the work site of those who support you. Not only do you want to send the message that you will be where the workers "work their magic," you want to learn what they do and how they do it. (What a great validation of your interest in each member of the staff and the sincerity of your desire to support each of them.)

Follow the head custodian around and ask him every question you can think of about the physical plant. Learn the inner workings of the building firsthand. You need to know everything from the placement of the fire extinguishers to the lighting and to how to work the public address system in the auditorium or cafeteria. No portion of each building should be strange to you. You will be a quick study because you don't have time to belabor tiny details. (After you understand how the physical plant operates in the entire school, then, and only then, will you be able to assign any part of this responsibility to someone else, such as an assistant principal, if there is one).

Next you'll meet with the food service staff. Imagine their surprise if you make that initial contact with a plate of cookies that they didn't have to make themselves.

If you couldn't get the bus drivers to meet with you, arrange a separate meeting that coincides with their schedules. Introduce yourself and get to know their names.

On the first day of school, go onto the bus with bottled water. Stop by the crossing guard with water as well—something to let them know you recognize and value their work.

Arrange monthly meetings with each subgroup. Monthly meetings will set the tone that this will be a team effort in supporting the school. Monthly meetings head off problems at the pass.

For additional sage advice, refer to Franzy Fleck's *What Successful Principals Do! 169 Tips for Principals* (2005). He offers helpful and practical suggestions on issues that confront the principal at the beginning, during, and end of the school year.

Organize your notes again. What group needs which issues resolved? You'll need the notes when you begin sorting out and prioritizing the problems to solve. Record the dates you identified for a follow-up meeting. If you plan to have another person take over a role with one of the groups, the new contact person will be in attendance for the follow-up meeting. You are working *smart*.

Are You Beginning to Feel Overwhelmed Already?

True Story

> I thought I was so prepared. But this job is really hard. There is just so much. I keep hoping it will get better.
>
> —High school assistant

As an administrator, you know you can become overwhelmed quickly. Not only do you have all the information you just gathered, but after meeting with your individuals and groups, you realize how many layers are forming. The vast amount of responsibilities that are yours could render you with information overload.

You don't want to develop "brain freeze" and begin fragmenting your time as a way to cope because you are trying to assimilate too much at one time. Keep telling yourself that you can't fix everything by next week. Nor is this the time to discount any piece of information as unnecessary or unimportant. Remember, this is not your history, but the history of many who came before you. Approach each issue methodically so that when you have something to fix, it is done in a smart, fast, and efficient way.

How will you know if you are overwhelmed? You could experience brain freeze at any time. How will you act? (See Appendix A.)

Questions and Answers

Q: Why should I take the time to meet with all of the people in noninstructional positions? In my big school, that will take a long time.

A: The most critical skill a principal needs is the ability to build trust and relationships between you and those who work with you. All staff members need to feel that you value them and the work they do. Noninstructional staff members often feel that they are overlooked and that the emphasis is on the teachers, not them. This is a time to dispel that belief. It is a lot of up-front time, but you'll be glad you took it.

Q: Monthly meetings? I don't have time for that. What's wrong with finding the problem and fixing it?

A: First, no one person can be expected to know how to solve everyone's problems. Any area that is not in your immediate experience level is unknown territory. Let the experts tell you how they think the identified problems can be resolved. If your combined efforts can't solve the problem, then at least they can provide you with enough background for you to get help from other sources. Staff members will feel especially valued when you ask their opinions.

Once you have a thorough understanding of everyone's needs and issues based on conversations and discussions with each of the identified groups. Then, and only then, can you assign someone else as the contact person because you understand the issues and will create realistic expectations about the task.

Survival Tips

Whatever you think, *never criticize your predecessor in any way.*

Do whatever you say you will do. Do it by the date you told the group or individual. You have hundreds of issues to keep track of (see Chapter 5). A group or individual has only one thing to remember—the one you said you would "look into" or "take care of." Trust begins when you do exactly what you said you would do. If it can't be done, then give a rationale and explain in person the reason why it can't or didn't happen. Avoidance does not make the issue go away.

Don't try to fix everything immediately. Many issues will come to your attention. Unless it causes obvious and immediate danger, wait to establish priorities when you have time to sort out the issues in a methodical rather than reactionary way. In older schools, multiple issues regarding facilities may have existed for years and could hold your time hostage. Record your findings. Wait until you talk to the resident expert about the history of the issue, the immediate need to fix it, and what can go on hold for the time being.

This is your mantra: "I've been studying the data and school information. Will you help me understand what I found?" End of story.

State only the facts as you know them—don't editorialize. A simple statement, even made under your breath to anyone that hears you, such as "I don't understand why these test scores are so low," immediately translates for the teachers into "That new principal doesn't think we're doing a good job, and I'll bet she makes us change everything." You didn't know that everything you say will now become reinterpreted and a matter of public record? It will.

You are a walking headline. Everything you say will be taken literally by those who hear you. School walls and halls have ears. Tread lightly and make no value judgments.

Get further training in understanding all of the elements of the school budget. Very few districts provide enough training in the budgets that relate to your specific school. You probably know the generic budgeting process. Ask the district expert for their time to work with your particular budget, including internal accounts, exceptional education, and funds for second-language learner programs. District experts are helpful and appreciate your asking. Experts want you to understand what to do. It makes their jobs easier than if you mess up and they have to fix it.

Know the source of money and the audit trails handled through student organizations and parent groups. Principals are held accountable for what happens to any money that comes through the doors of the school or handled as part of an organization. Learn the procedures and audit processes. Check with your supervisor and ask for permission to order an audit trail as soon as you assume your assignment. Sit with someone in charge of the money in the district and review the audit.

True Story

> As principal, I stayed out of the details of the Parent Teacher Organization. We had a dedicated group of parents, competent, and hard-working. I should have stuck my nose into their work and pushed for an audit at the end of each year. It turns out thousands of dollars were unaccounted for over the years. Everyone assumed that the books had been audited. They weren't. It was years before it was straightened out.
>
> —High school principal

Ask for help. Every supervisor and veteran master principal understands what it was like to be the new one. Don't let your ego or insecurities get in the way of asking for advice from the experts. It is efficient and smart and saves tons of time.

Summary

This chapter has covered the time frame from the beginning of your appointment until the teachers arrive. Often the information in this chapter occurs can be gathered in six weeks to two months, if you were appointed during the summer.

Throughout this chapter and other chapters to follow, there are references to *off-the-clock time* spent on tedious tasks such as dissecting test data. The only concentrated time you have will be when everyone is gone from the school or when you take the work home. This becomes off the clock time.

As the principal, you face constant interruptions during the time that staff occupies the campus. You must be available to them when they need you. This is *on-the-clock* time. The first year requires more off-the-clock time than you may expect. The new principal is smart, fast and efficient in his or her analysis. Without a methodical approach to understanding your school, you can easily exhibit behaviors symptomatic of one who acts completely overwhelmed. This chapter described behaviors that principals and assistant principals demonstrate when they are overloaded with information and resort to avoidance behavior as a way to cope (see Appendix A).

As a new principal or assistant, you must recognize when you begin experiencing avoidance behaviors. You need to take a deep breath, step back, and review the recommendations presented. Even if no one mentions it, these meltdown behaviors do not go unnoticed by staff, students, and parents. It may seem odd that feeling overwhelmed happens so early in your appointment. It can. However, it also can be avoided through a study of the issues and a plan to work with priorities.

Even when you feel prepared for the assignment, it is an overwhelming feeling to realize that you are now the one in charge, and there is a lot to accomplish before school begins. If you are appointed during the school year, the challenge is even greater because the same tasks must be accomplished while you are learning what makes the school tick. Either way, your "need to know" regarding important school information is the same and must be accomplished in the same order

Before school begins, examine the facts in the following sequence:

1. Start when you examine and analyze existing school data on student performance, demographics, and staff background.

2. Develop a system to categorize your findings as you review available information on your new school.

3. Create lists of questions to ask yourself and others.

4. Discuss your findings with key people identified within the chapter.

5. Analyze your own experiences and leadership style, reflect continuously on how your style and belief system fit into the current culture.

6. Examine your own background experiences in curriculum, instruction, and assessment. Stay objective.

7. Remain in a questioning and reflecting mode throughout your investigation and discussion.

Reflections

1. What are the ways that a principal could work smart and efficiently when analyzing test data?

2. What advantages do you see in spending time with the various individuals and groups as a way to further understand the inner workings of the school? What could be the result if you didn't meet with groups?

3. Discuss and describe various strategies for taking notes, organizing them, and creating your system that could provide an efficient way to access the information when you need it.

4. What would you do if you found glaring discrepancies between the data you analyzed and individual groups' perceptions of what happens in their school?

5. New principals and assistant principals are reluctant to ask for help because they worry that someone may think they are not capable of doing the job. Do you agree or disagree with this premise? Explain.

6. Discuss as many problems as you can imagine if you do not understand the details of the budget. In what ways could you work efficiently and still keep track of budget issues?

3

Establishing a Collaborative Environment: I Am Now an Administrator—I Have Keys, I Have an Office. But Where Am I?

(One Month before the Teachers Arrive)

By now, your head is spinning from the number of notes you took and the temporary conclusions you reached as you began establishing timelines for district deadlines, reflected on your personal background, analyzed data, and met with people. By now, you realize the history of the school and the underlying issues that created the school that you will lead.

You hold all the pieces of the puzzle. The puzzle is still just that—a puzzle. You are far from making a complete picture at this point. In this chapter, you will focus on the beginning of putting puzzle pieces together.

The administrator of a complex organization called a school requires the help of others. A Leadership Team becomes the first step in establishing the connection between what you learned in your investigations and a group of staff members who can assist you. They help you make the critical connections between past practices and the direction you will take when leading the school for the first time.

Understanding the culture and your ability to embed your beliefs and personality in your new environment requires considerable study. Examining the culture requires analysis of the internal culture in which you will work throughout the day and the external culture that exists in the school community as a whole. Both cultures are important and affect how the school operates. Seymour Sarason's *Revisiting "The Culture of the School and the Problem of Change"* (1996) describes the complex process of understanding and working within the school culture.

Time is still your most valuable commodity—use it wisely. On-the-clock time is spent with people, not things. Arrange your office and the contents of your desk on the weekend during off-the-clock time (see Chapter 5). Take a deep breath; you have a lot to do. Teachers will be arriving soon. Students will arrive soon after that.

 ## When Do I Begin?

One month before the first official welcome-back staff meeting, you will begin connecting your temporary conclusions with those who have a history with the school.

Members of the staff who have been at the school for three or more years have information concerning how and why the culture is the way it is, understand the student and parent population, and understand the rationale for decisions made by teaching teams and your predecessor. It is not necessary for the team members to be the kings and queens of the school—the members just need an objective perspective (Manz & Sims, 2001).

You have formed some of your own conclusions by now. This is the time when you have enough background information to start putting it all together. You continue to ask probing questions of those who can provide you answers regarding the current state of the school and what expectations the staff may possess about the plans for the upcoming year. This is a smart and efficient way to get important questions answered.

What Should I Do and How Should I Do It?

Identify members of the school who serve in an advisory capacity to the principal. The staff members may constitute a Leadership Team that already functioned in that role during your predecessor's term. There is an assumption that this is a group of school leaders who represent other members of the staff. This group should comprise a cross-section of school leaders. Often, they are the team or department leaders. They understand the workings of the school and provide valuable insight regarding the history of the school.

Identify a way to compensate the members for meeting with you. You should plan on a full day to meet with your group. Of course, provide food. Call or write to each member inviting them to participate. Because everyone is not always available during the summer, you may have to be satisfied with fewer numbers than usually comprise the team.

Numbers on the Leadership Team depend on the size of the school. Smaller schools may have only a guidance counselor and principal's secretary. Other schools also may have an assistant and a curriculum person. Large schools also may have additional specialists.

The Leadership Team Meeting, Part I

Purpose

The purpose of the Leadership Team meeting is fourfold:

1. Review your findings from the hard data.
2. Discuss the findings you gathered from the people you met with (described in Chapters 1 and 2).
3. Identify the key issues to approach during the coming school year.
4. Plan for the beginning of school.

Create an agenda with very specific time frames for discussion. These members of the staff are busy, and you want to set a tone for working smarter, not harder. Start on time, keep to the agenda, and end on time. Put on your cheeriest personality. This will not be the forum to fuss about anything. You will present the facts as you found them. Discuss them one at a time.

As part of the agenda, agree on confidentiality. Ask the teams for their perceptions of your information. If there are specific items that should be shared with the staff, then make sure everyone knows what you will say and ask for the team's help. Ask, "How do you think this should be handled with the staff?"

Find someone on the staff—a secretary, clerk, assistant principal, or media specialist—who can serve as recording secretary. Take your own notes and encourage others to do the same. When the meeting is over, this recollection serves a purpose for later discussions and a review of the minutes.

Discuss the Perceptions You Received from the Contacts You Made Earlier

Start with the positive perceptions others gave. For example, repeat your predecessor's statement: "I will really enjoy working with this staff, everyone is so cooperative." Watch the body language on this one. Information generated from such comments could save you months of time figuring out if there are hidden issues with some staff members. At a time like this, you'll hear a lot. This could guide the way you develop your personal plan to lead the school. (Just make sure you keep the information confidential—if any part of what the Leadership Team said to you makes its way to the uninformed, you are "dead meat.")

Another example is, "My supervisor tells me how professional all of you are. You demonstrate a very high quality as educators. I'm impressed. I am so lucky to be working with you." (This is the type of "'attaboy" compliment that can be shouted from the rooftops.) Staff members need all the positive accolades possible. Perceptions drive reality. If the Leadership Team hears how positive you are about the school, the word will spread.

True Story

> The staff had experienced a lot of turnover of administrators over the past few years. I overheard one teacher saying to the other, "I don't care what she says, I did what I do before she got here, and I'll do what I do after she is gone." So the first thing I said every time I got a chance—"They will have to carry me out of here feet first. I am in this for the long haul." A couple of the old-timers almost had a cardiac arrest.
>
> —Middle school principal

Review the Data with Your Team

Discuss one area at a time: subjects, grade levels, and any other portion of the data you analyzed. As you proceed through the data, ask more questions than you give answers. You are still on a fact-finding mission, but now you will ask others to clarify your findings.

People with history at the school often can explain the unexplainable. For example, you found that one 10th-grade teacher's students, on the whole, obtained very low standardized test scores relative to the expectations for her class of Advanced Placement students. The Leadership Team might tell you about the extenuating circumstances of the students during the year. Perhaps they may had three teachers during the year, or there may have been a tragedy with one of the classmates one week before testing. There may be no explanation other than poor teaching. (Make a note to check out this perception. Did your predecessor mention this teacher?)

You noticed that a sixth-grade teacher's students, on the whole, received significantly lower scores on their tests than other students at the same grade level. The Leadership Team may explain that this class was added in January and comprised students who came later in the year. Most of them had been at the school for only three months before the standardized testing occurred. (You ask and make a note about the procedures for adding classrooms after the school year begins and the process for placement of students.)

Another teacher's students improved significantly over other classes in the same grade. He is doing something that works. What is it?

Review the written School Improvement Plan for the year, if there is one. Ask about any procedures or plans that address the data you found. For example, you examined the discrepancy among different ethnic groups. Were there any plans to do something with this information? Ask the team for their understanding of the remedy, if there was one planned.

Discussions with the Leadership Team Get to the Underlying Issues

This is the time to discuss the philosophy of the school and the goals the school is trying to reach, irrespective of test scores. For example, perhaps the school implemented a bully prevention program. The team can explain the details of this program. You would then ask why it was necessary to implement the program. Perhaps you forgot to examine the suspension and expulsions rates when you were knee-deep in test scores. (Make a note.)

Another important issue to investigate concerns the difference between what you see as the major concerns and the conclusions you reached from your predecessor. One would hope that there is no discrepancy. If there is, proceed cautiously. The Leadership Team is the group that can help you understand how far any change of plans can go during your first year. Whether or not you agree, listen. Their insight will become significant as you determine your next steps.

The involvement of the parents and their impact on the school is also important background information. It's keep-this-confidential time, and responses are off the record. Frequently, staff members are parts of different parent groups and have unique insight. Some parents' groups have been a part of the culture for a long time and have established their presence in one form or the other. You want to find out as much information about these issues as possible so that you won't be caught off guard when you meet them as a group for the first time.

If you are uncomfortable asking staff members the questions below, move these questions to your discussion with your predecessor or your assistant (if you have one).

- Which parent groups have real power?
- Which parent groups have perceived power?
- Within the groups who are the supporters?
- Within the groups who or where are the challenges?
- In the past, what was the relationship between each of the groups and the administration?
- If parents are not very involved, what are the reasons?

True Story

I'll never forget the first time I met parents in my new school. It was a school that had been in existence for a long time. Two parents came up to me and said, "It is old money here you know my dear." I'm thinking, "What does that mean?" It's those same parents that later were busted because they were buying stolen designer handbags from the back of a van. You've got to love it.

—Middle school assistant

Create a "Top Three to Tackle" List

- You discussed the data, engaged in discussions concerning this year's plan for school improvement, or you realize that one needs creating.

- Review the highlights of the information and move to the next step.
- Ask the Leadership Team to brainstorm each of the issues that needs your immediate attention. List them on a chart. This is not redundant. It simply narrows the focus and makes your job more manageable.
- You are the first person to really examine the issues. This information may reveal new issues to address. This is the time to reveal any concerns and good news that you may unearth.
- Identify the top three issues, in order of importance, that you and the team agree need attention. When you are new to the school, you can handle only the most glaring concerns. You will save the complete list and review the other concerns later on in the year. But for now, bite off only what you can chew successfully, or you are in for one major stomachache.
- Identify the solutions and people who could help you with the resolutions.
- Summarize the findings as you review the minutes taken during this meeting.

Keep the Staff Informed at All Times

As principal, you will review the minutes from the Leadership Team and send copies to everyone on the Leadership Team for review. They will send their edited versions back to you. You, in turn, will remove any of the confidential statements made.

Every member of the staff should receive a final copy: a hard copy, a copy by e-mail, and a copy during preplanning. This informs people, keeps them up to speed on the decisions being made, and describes proposed suggestions. This sets an important tone. Everyone will be informed about the decisions being made and why. Staff members who enjoy speculating and spreading contrived stories about what might happen in the school now that you are there—and why—will be quickly deterred because everyone knows the same information.

The importance of distributing minutes of all meetings to all members of the staff and finding underlying issues within a school is discussed in *Case Studies in Constructivist Leadership and Teaching* by Arthur Shapiro (2003).

There is no need to include the following section in the minutes. Planning for the beginning of the school year could include the same or different staff members depending on the time available. The purpose is the same.

Leadership Team Meeting, Part II (Same Day)

Plan for Your First Staff Meeting— An Event vs. "Sit and 'Git"

The following examples are based on the presumption that teachers begin at least two days before school starts to get things set up. Ask the team to explain the procedures the first time teachers meet with you, the principal. Review the previous year's schedule. The answers usually vary from one extreme to the other.

Teachers may arrive, maybe have coffee and juice, sit down, and hear the principal give a "rah-rah" speech and a lecture on school procedures. Then teachers receive the new handbooks and a to-do list, and everyone goes on their merry way to do what they have always done. (This usually leaves the new teachers with a deer-in-the-headlights look of confusion.)

Or, teachers could arrive at an event. There is a well-defined theme around which the meeting area is designed. Teachers feel the tone of the new school year. Something is new here, and it feels good. New teachers meet with you again to review procedures and to receive additional support that veteran teachers don't need.

Theme-Driven Preplanning Days

If you can convince the team that this is a time to establish a theme that will drive the rest of the year, it may be the start of your informal leadership. Ask, "What slogan, or theme, would demonstrate our objectives for the year?" If they have an idea, great! Perhaps they want to play off a goal from last year. An issue generated during the Leadership Team meeting might provide a springboard for an idea.

If this is a new concept or they can't think of anything, here is another example. As principal, you want to establish team building or school unity as your personal goal. Based on the information you gathered, you see this as a need. Ask, "Do you think that team building is a good goal for this coming year?" Most staff members see this as a continuous need. You solicit their support, but in the end, it is something you plan to do. Keep it a surprise for the rest of the staff.

- ◆ It doesn't take any more time for the teachers to arrive at an event than to arrive at a business-as-usual sit and 'git. But as the new principal, is that what you want? Assume you would like something different. Set a different tone—from "I'm the boss, so here is what you have to do" to "We are in this together, so let's build a team. I want you, as the staff, to feel how much I value you."

- You want teachers to arrive for their first day in an environment that makes each one of them feel like a true professional, just like the corporate people.

- Because few people will be available to help you before school starts, you have work ahead of you. There is a lot to collect and organize: Scrounge for parent and business support and find some money for the supplies. Make this an efficient process, work within a reasonable budget, and assign tasks to get as much help as possible. Do the things that time and money allow. If you are very lucky, some of your office staff will rally around your idea and help.

- Create a theme that translates into the nonthreatening tone you want to set. Here is one example: "Together We Will Build Success." This is a generic theme that shouldn't send anyone over the edge worrying about you, the new guy or gal.

- What does that look like? *Build* is the operative word. The tables are covered with drop cloths, the team wears hardhats to greet the staff on the first day, each staff member has a small paint bucket filled with their office supplies (including rulers), their name tags have a building-type logo on them, ladders decorate the meeting area. Creativity is rampant.

- Rather than boring lectures, teachers can read. Show a short video that promotes team building. This is a nice segue for you as principal and your assistant (if you have one) to describe how you want to support teachers in their efforts to develop teams that *Build for Success* for themselves and their students. Hopefully, a technology or media specialist can help you out.

- Any other idea works the same way. What's the theme? How can you show what it looks like and sounds like? How can you use the theme in your initial speech (2–3 minutes)? How can you continue the theme throughout the year? Teachers may want to use the same theme on their teams or in their classrooms.

- Do you think this is too hokey for secondary teachers? Try it. You might be surprised. The time spent with the staff is the same, it just looks and feels different.

- Your discussion of the beginning of school and your desire to demonstrate that every teacher is a professional sets the tone with the team and for your desire to work together with the staff. The word will spread from your Leadership Team. They may even be willing to help you get the event together.

Find a Buddy, a Mentor, and a Coach

The Role of a Mentor as Coach

You may be pretty insecure about your findings from the preliminary data you gathered and need a perception check. You want to do the right thing, but you're not sure what that is. You ask your mentor for his or her coaching.

Who makes a good mentor? Large districts often assign a mentor who may or may not be a good match for you. They may not have any more experience than you. That person may be in your fall-back position, but you may need someone else.

You need a mentor who is also a coach. What is the difference? A mentor can provide support and needed explanations about technical things that a principal needs to do, forms to complete, deadlines to meet, and issues of principal protocol. A coach is someone with the experience to explain what to say to the extremely crabby parent; help you with the language for your personal improvement plan assigned by your supervisor; and how to take the short path toward getting your school facilities addressed. A coach can give you the in-depth understanding of your job. This person is a valuable connection.

- You need someone who has experience at your school level: elementary, middle, or high school. It doesn't have to be someone you even know that well, but they must have an excellent reputation. Just ask. You'll be surprised at how willing your colleagues are to help. Everyone was new at some time.

- Recently retired principals are an often-forgotten resource. They are willing to help if you just ask. You may know one from the district whom you respect.

- What did you think of your predecessor? Is he or she willing to coach you? Did you feel a connection with your predecessor?

- Refer to your notes from your meeting with your supervisor. Check out the recommendation for a mentor. Does your supervisor see the mentor as a coach? You can't do this job without someone to ask the hard questions and give reasonable suggestions. Your support group is a very small network compared to your former teacher support groups. You need someone.

- Sometimes you can locate the resident principal expert. This is the person who, during management meetings or your association meetings, says the smart things and seems to have a pretty good grasp of the local issues. Don't be shy. Ask this person if he or she would mind a call them from time to time to ask questions. He or she will be glad to help. Principals are in the helping business. That's what they do. Then, call them—ask. This is working smart.

The Role of a Buddy

- This is a quick answer if you have worked in the district where you received your appointment. You have already found a buddy.
- A buddy may not know any more than you do about the job. Buddies serve the function of a shoulder to cry on or a person you trust to share your frustrations. They just need a lot of empathy for what you do and what you go through on a daily basis.
- Buddies may not even be in education. But they do need to keep your confidence. There are many things that should be for their ears only. You just need to vent, and vent you will.
- Buddies may serve a dual role, mentor and buddy. This is usually a principal friend.

Meet with Parent Groups

- The size of the school will dictate the number of parent groups that are in the school.
- Which groups generate money? Refer back to your notes from the meeting with the bookkeeper, discussed in Chapter 2. Do you remember how individual groups control their money? Make sure you know exactly how the audit trail works for each group.
- Arrange a meeting with all of the groups at one time. Because your time is so crunched, one strategy may be a breakfast meeting at which, upon receiving an invitation, any parent on a committee can join you for an informal get-together. Involved parents want to meet you. Plan something like a "Meet the Principal Coffee Get-Together." (By now you will have this tea party thing down to a fine science. Don't give up on the idea, it works.)
- Ask members of the office to create a list of the heads of each parent group and contact them to meet with you. Large schools may only have space for the officers of each organization. Small schools may want to meet with more parents. Keep the numbers manageable.

Parents want to know your position on issues you have no clue about at this point. You become the target for every issue they couldn't get past your predecessor. This puts your public relations charm to the test.

The answer to parent inquiries: "Please send me the issues as you see them. If you write them down and give them to me, send them by mail, or e-mail, I will then be better prepared to respond. I know I'll have questions to ask as well. Also, include the date of your group's next meeting. I'll be there. In that way we can make the most out of our time together." It also takes you off the hot seat for the moment. This is both smart and efficient.

Requesting the issues ahead of time gives you some think time. It also gives you a chance to find out the story behind the story from someone on campus who understands each of the various committees.

During an earlier discussion with the bookkeeper, you learned how money is generated by individual groups, including the important audit trail. Compare the official requirements for parent handling of money to the practice. Don't be surprised if reality and practice are different.

When working in schools of poverty and schools with little or no parent involvement, work with your supervisor and predecessor to explore ways that worked in the past to get parent involvement. What does your supervisor expect of you? You know that parent participation is important, but what is realistic?

Learning the Culture

You are getting more of a flavor for the culture of the school. This is one of the most important parts of your job as a new administrator, and perhaps the most complicated. Understanding the culture by adapting to your new environment becomes critically important to your success.

Culture can be described as the way the school does business. It involves an understanding of the stakeholders. Culture exists because of the history and evolution of the school. Among the many authors who write about school cultures, Michael Fullan's *Leading in a Culture of Change* (2001) explains the importance of recognizing and understanding the role of cultures within a school.

Thinking about the factors that determine the culture you are entering may give you the "hmmm" during conversations with veteran staff members and parents. No reactive comments, just "hmmm."

As principal and assistant principal, drive around the community your school serves. What do you see? Describe the environment. How do you feel? Now, ask the hard questions of yourself to think about the culture of the school and how will you fit into the new culture:

- What is your personal background in relation to this school? Is this similar to or different from the cultures where you grew up or went to high school or college? How might that affect your expectations for teaching and learning?

- ◆ What is your personal background from the last school at which you were employed? Is this similar to or different from the culture of the last school where you worked?
- ◆ Do either of the two previous backgrounds come close to those that you think exist in your new school? What is the same? What is different?
- ◆ How do you think parents perceive their role in relation to the school? Not involved? Sometimes involved? Overly involved?
- ◆ How does the school accommodate the special needs of the children? Are teachers committed to an inclusion model? Are there programs to serve needs of specific groups of children? Are there programs designed for specific reasons, other than those expected because of state requirements?
- ◆ What ethnic backgrounds affect how the school does business?
- ◆ How do the ethnic backgrounds affect how the school does business?
- ◆ What are the teachers' expectations of the administrator? ___Leave me alone. ___I want to learn. ___Tell me what to do.
- ◆ What are the teachers' expectations of the students? ___We teach, they learn. ___We provide strategies so that students can learn to think, solve problems, and make thoughtful decisions.
- ◆ How many years has this school operated? What difference does that make?
- ◆ Is the community a stable one? If so, and the school has functioned in this environment for years, did the current students' parents attend this same school? What difference does that make? If not, is the community in transition, newer, younger families, different cultures, or changing socioeconomic structures?
- ◆ Is this a new community, built in a new subdivision, or a section of the city or town? If so, how does this affect the culture?
- ◆ What other questions should you ask? List them in your notes.

True Story

I am obviously white. When an African American dad was enrolling his daughter at the school his three-year old, who was with him, started yelling at his dad and pointing at me saying, "Daddy, Daddy, look at this lady, she is really white. How come she is so white?" His dad was so embarrassed. I just went over to them and I said, "Yes, when God made me he got carried away with white." I held the child's hands, then he touched my blonde hair. Dad and I both had a good laugh. I think when the little one left, he was still confused. I love the diversity of our school.

—Elementary teacher-leader

Understand the External and Internal Culture

Within each community, there is an informal structure that defines parent and community expectations about the school. Where are they, and how can you find them? Begin by asking members of the staff, who are also members of the community, key questions. Where could you find groups of your parents where conversation about school probably occurs?

- Church? Is there one church that becomes the hub?
- Baseball, soccer, or football fields?
- 4-H?
- Grocery store (between the milk and potatoes)?
- Bowling alley?
- Homeowners' association?
- Women's league?
- Rotary or Kiwanis Club?
- Chamber of commerce?
- Adult sorority and fraternity organizations?

Should you hang out there? Join the club? It may not be necessary, but it is important to know the source of parent-generated information. Teachers who are also active members of these groups can be great with public relations about the positive issues at the school.

Examine the Inner Workings of the School Culture Relative to Instruction, Curriculum, and Assessment

Evaluate the difference between your personal beliefs about curriculum, instruction, and current practices within the school. You may lean toward a traditional school of thought. What does that mean?

- Drill and practice sheets are the tools of choice in skill acquisition.
- Students rarely participate in cooperative groups or group work.
- Experiences in learning come from projects with low-level thinking outcomes.
- Teacher's manuals are highly scripted, and teachers depend on a single textbook-driven curriculum.
- Textbooks are specifically purchased to provide a teacher-centered environment.
- Homework is given with little apparent purpose.
- Letter grading is strict and nonnegotiable.
- Projects are generally completed at home, with low-level thinking expectations.
- Instruction concentrates on skill building.
- There is a strict tracking system for students, with clear distinctions made among groups because of their academic achievement.
- At the elementary level, student placement in classes is permanent and based on assigned level of ability to learn—the Buzzards, Bluebirds, and Eagles reading and math grouping phenomenon.
- Placement of students in specific tracks is defined according to their standardized test scores.

Is this the culture of the school to which you are now assigned? Is this your philosophy? If so, nothing will change, and you will be very comfortable. This means everyone is satisfied with the level of student progress. (Aren't you the lucky one?) The transition from your philosophy to a school with the same philosophy existing in a culture that supports it will be relatively easy.

Perhaps you have a more experiential, constructivist, or concept-based philosophy concerning student learning. What does that mean in terms of your personal philosophy and whether it is consistent with the existing instructional practices at your new school?

- Teachers examine individual and group needs, adjusting their skill instruction to the situation as necessary to support additional instruction.

- Students often learn through discussion and higher-order thinking in cooperative learning situations and small groups.
- Project-based learning provides specific and thorough learning through an in-depth study of a particular subject. Students work independently on this activity with teacher guidance at school, not as homework.
- Well-designed rubrics identify student-assessment criteria.
- Higher-order thinking, problem solving, and decision making dominate instructional strategies.
- Student placement in class is based on a matrix that defines multiple criteria for placement or a clearly defined placement plan, as opposed to a single standardized test score.
- Multiple genres provide opportunities for students to engage in thoughtful discussions concerning literature across the content areas.

You may describe your own beliefs as a combination of both belief systems. Does it match your findings from the discussion with the Leadership Team? What do you believe? What are your beliefs regarding how you want the school to function for teachers, students, and parents, described in Chapter 1?

The Assistant Principal's Role

As the assistant principal, you have an important responsibility on several levels. Your role is to do the following:

- Serve as a member of the Leadership Team. As such, you provide valuable insight into the history of the school and the path taken so far.
- Support the principal and help to avoid unnecessary conflicts.
- Serve as a resource.
- Adjust to a new personality, leadership style, and vision.
- Remain flexible.
- Learn from your new boss. If you want to achieve the same level as principal, you need to study the steps a new principal takes. You may be there some day.
- Step back from your current assignments and let the new principal determine your role. More than likely, it will remain the same.
- Ask questions to clarify your role and the principal's expectations.

- Keep the principal informed of all issues, concerns, and activities when they come to your attention.
- Help the principal to work efficiently.
- Complete the tasks assigned, on time and with the highest level of competence..

Your role is not to do the following:

- Rescue or overshadow the principal.
- Promote your own personal agenda.
- Overstep your boundaries just because there is a new principal around who still may be overcoming a learning curve.
- Decide you are in charge while waiting for the new boss to get up to speed.
- Undermine the decisions of the principal because you know the way it is "supposed" to be done.
- Assume anything the principal may think, feel, or determine important without asking.

Questions and Answers

Q: Why do I need to meet with the Leadership Team a full month before the teachers come back?

A: First, you need their feedback on your findings. Otherwise, you may jump to unwarranted conclusions and waste your time developing unnecessary plans. Second, regardless of whether you are planning on a theme for your first meeting with the staff, you need their suggestions on how to organize the first week with teachers. You need to maintain the structure teachers are used to for the first year. Otherwise, you set the tone that you plan to change everything. Of course you don't, but it doesn't take much for teachers to think that you will. Be patient. Your time will come.

Q: Once I get a feel for the school, will I have all these meetings with small groups every year in the middle of the summer?

A: Probably not, you may be able to accomplish the same thing in the spring when you begin planning the following year's schedule.

Q: I've just been assigned to a high-risk school. I want the challenge, but I haven't heard anything positive from the central office about the school. What should I say to the Leadership Team?

A: Even if the results are not the ones the central office wants, teachers in high-risk schools want to be there, or they would be somewhere else.

Say something such as "I recognize that we have challenges to meet. I know you are dedicated and committed to help the students here or you would have selected another school. We can work through this together. It will happen because of your support." This is a time to build on everything positive and analyze the things that need fixing very carefully.

Q: It seems as if this theme thing is a bit much. It's a lot of work. What's the point?

A: The experiences of veteran principals support the idea that teachers frequently complain that they don't feel as if they are treated like professionals. Who better to set that tone than you? You can demonstrate that you view each staff member as a professional and will treat them as such. Staff members should be made to feel important and valued. Strange as it may seem, an event makes a positive first impression about you and the tone you set from the beginning. It is worth the effort.

Q: The democratic approach involving Leadership Teams and minutes going out to everyone is very time-consuming. Yet, I have to work smart, fast, and efficient—but this isn't fast.

A: This approach emphasizes working smart. It is time intensive up front. However, meetings don't have to take hours and hours. You will model for your Leadership Team and others how to set a tight agenda, keep to the point, provide members an opportunity to examine options, draw specific conclusions, and provide time for feedback. You also will model the importance of examining all of the information concerning an issue, involving the stakeholders that could be affected by a decision, and drawing informed conclusions. Everyone on the staff should be well informed at all times.

Q: What should I do if I am appointed during the year?

A: Modify each of the recommended stages. The greatest challenge is finding the time to carefully analyze the data to draw conclusions about how to proceed once school starts. Your off-the-clock time will probably expand. You will go from one issue to another with lightening speed once the teachers and students are at school full time.

If you are appointed in January or later, you will work from a plan developed for next year. For the time being, you will keep this year's ship afloat. All of the suggested steps noted previously will be implemented with the upcoming year in mind.

 **Survival Tips**

If you decide to develop a theme, make sure you don't change the amount of time spent on this activity compared to the time staff members have spent in the past. For example, if the staff has always taken one hour on the first day back to "sit and 'git," then have your event last just one hour. This can change over the years, but not now. You can continue the theme throughout the year. It's the initial impression that lasts with staff, whether it's for one hour, one day, or several days.

Hint: One of your buddies and you can develop two different themes, one at each school during the same year. You gather all of the "stuff" for the theme, props, table decorations, etc. Then, next year exchange your themes. If you keep the themes generic enough, they can be adapted for any emphasis. This strategy saves a lot of time for the subsequent year. (OK, so year three you start all over or find a third person.)

Send a letter to each member of the staff welcoming him or her back. The letter can emphasize your theme as you introduce yourself. The letter concludes with the questions detailed in Chapter 6. You ask the typical information for the school files, but add the names of the people living in the house and the names of pets.

Everyone on the staff should receive copies of all minutes from all meetings. The domino effect that occurs when you, your Leadership Team, grade level, department, or ad hoc teams or groups make decisions can be very upsetting to other members of the staff who may be affected. Generally, the support groups are the last to know of a decision or change in schedule. Media, guidance, custodial, exceptional education, second-language programs, physical education, music, and food preparation people are often the last to know of a decision or change in schedules or events that could ultimately affect them. E-mail is an efficient delivery method if it is available. The greatest benefit occurs when, as principal and assistant, you and all other staff members know what happened at each meeting. There are no surprises to you or others about what is occurring throughout the school.

If the staff chooses not to read the minutes, so be it. This method of communication eliminates speculation about what you may or may not be doing and keeps everyone informed. This is an especially helpful solution to the rumor mill in large schools, where information becomes highly distorted as it passes from mouth to mouth across dozens of people. More important, it provides a method for staff to head off conflict about schedule or procedures at the pass.

This is another helpful reference for the newsletter that goes to the staff. This contains otherwise overlooked or unknown information because the person who writes the weekly bulletin can refer to the minutes as reference.

Keep the schedule of meetings the same during the first two months as principal. If the staff usually meets for one hour on the first day of preplanning, meet for one hour. You will change to your schedule later on as you work with the Leadership Team and decide how to alter meeting times so that you can begin making your mark.

Before you change schedules, ask a couple of staff members who have a reputation for being neurotic about organization and detail, "If we changed the schedule from this to this, what effect would that have on the school?" They will tell you and save you mountains of grief. At the elementary level, ask a kindergarten teacher; at the middle and high school level, ask the media specialist or administrative secretary.

Summary

This chapter described the importance of establishing a Leadership Team. As a new principal, you need people around you who can provide you with the historical connection of past practices. From that information, you and your Leadership Team can identify the top three issues to tackle for the remainder of the year.

Every staff member should become accustomed to receiving minutes and information from all meetings. They may not read them, but they can't say they didn't know what was going on. E-mail is an efficient way to get information out quickly, but a photocopy is just fine.

Utilizing a theme approach to create an event for your staff during your initial meeting can set an important tone. You are able to demonstrate your commitment to a goal within a professional environment. Teachers love "stuff." When you provide free things to teachers, described in this chapter, you immediately gain staff points.

New principals and assistant principals are notorious for trying to solve problems themselves. They do not seek help from others for several different reasons: (1) They fear that someone will think they can't do the job; (2) they believe they know everything they need to know; (3) they have no idea what they need to ask; or (4) it is faster.

This chapter suggested that other administrators in the organization are willing and able to assist new principals with any questions or concerns. A principal who does not ask questions is a principal who spends too much time trying to figure things out on their own, wasting time, and definitely not working efficiently.

Understanding the culture of a school is a critical component for a new principal. The school has a culture that is defined on a variety of levels. There is an external culture; this culture is found where parents and students congregate in large groups. School is often the topic of conversation. Every school community has such an external culture. The principal and assistant should understand where the parent groups form, such as specific sports events, church, music groups, scouts, 4-H, bowling, the country club, the chamber of commerce, and other places. A conscious decision should be made regarding how much the administrator participates in the external culture.

There is also an inner school culture. The impact of the community on the school becomes part of the school culture. The impact of cultures, past teaching practices, educational expectations of the veteran teachers and parents, as well as the previous administrator define the inner culture.

The principal enters these cultures as an outsider. It is up to the administrator to understand and live with the existing culture at this point. However, the caveat is when something is just plain intolerable and really pushes your buttons. Just be careful in how you approach your personal issues. Unless it is a situation that involves the health or safety of all members of the school, the issue may wait until you have a firmer handle on the culture.

Reflections

1. Assume you do not like the idea of a theme and event to welcome teachers back to school. However, you agree that setting a tone sends the message that, as principal, you will treat everyone as a professional. What would your welcome back to school look like?

2. Assuming that you would use the existing Leadership Team to help you get a handle on the school, how would you assess the ef-

fectiveness of the team? Use a scenario that describes a team you consider ineffective. What would you do?

3. Discuss the pros and cons of sending copies of the minutes of group meetings to everyone on the staff. What would you do, and why? Do you think there is a better way of keeping everyone informed? What would it be?

4. Describe in detail the culture of your school. By what criteria do you determine the characteristics of the culture?

5. If you were appointed in January or later in the school year, what would you do differently than if you were appointed during the summer? Explain how you would modify each of the steps.

4

Expecting and Handling the Unimaginable: Crisis vs. Conflict—Triage and Bandages

(First Two Months on the Job)

A crisis or a conflict requires two different leadership approaches. It is likely that your predecessor's leadership style was very different from yours. During your first few months at the school, the staff will watch you like a hawk, wondering how you will react to just about everything and comparing you with the style they know. All the staff will wonder how you handle a crisis compared to how you deal with a conflict.

In a crisis, the leader can emerge as someone racing around with no apparent direction or respond utilizing a hospital emergency triage system. Crisis occurs when the unexpected, unimaginable, and often incomprehensible event blindsides a school leader. It can happen the first day of school.

Conflict exists consistently and predictably. Decisions are made continuously in a school organization, and not all stakeholders will agree with the decisions. Conflict can develop between parents and teachers, between teachers and teachers, between students and teachers, and between administrators and any of the stakeholders when a problem remains unresolved.

Schools are no longer immune from crisis. In the past, principals sympathized with occurrences of crisis when they happened in *that other school*. Few could empathize. Principals and assistant principals would say, "I feel so sorry for the school administrators who dealt with that terrible event" while secretly thinking, "Thank God it wasn't me." That was then, and this is now. No one is immune. Elementary, middle, and high schools, rural and urban, must plan for catastrophic events. As the principal and assistant principal, you must be prepared.

As an administrator, what should you do and how should you act in anticipation of an unexpected and tragic event at your school? What should you do and how should you act when you experience a conflict between you and another person or group or between members of your staff or parent groups.

When Do I Begin?

As soon as you receive your appointment and for the next two months, you will prepare an effective personal and schoolwide plan.

◆ Examine your own personal behavior during a crisis.

◆ Become mentally prepared. Recognize that you may have to operate outside your comfort level.

◆ Examine the documents currently in place at your school and at the district level that describe how you should respond to a catastrophic event.

◆ Create a Crisis Response Team.

◆ Develop or revise a catastrophic strategic plan.

You must be prepared from the beginning of your assignment. Crisis will not wait for you to get settled into a routine. In some cases, crisis occurs within the first weeks of school. Principals who lived through the tragedy of September 11, in New York, four back-to-back hurricanes the during first two months of school in Florida in 2004, or the Gulf Coast hurricanes in 2005 can attest to this fact.

Examine Your Own Behavior under Pressure

Think about a time when you experienced a personal crisis, such as a car accident or a serious injury to your child. How did you react? Will this behavior determine how you will react in the school setting? Did you freeze, unable to move? Did you panic and start running around with no apparent plan? Did you start yelling at everyone around you? Did you rise to the occasion and worry about your own needs later?

What is the only behavior that is acceptable in a time of crisis? Leadership behavior requires thoughtful, clear thinking and triage behavior. Essentially, you must act as though you are chief of staff in a major hospital and dozens of patients need immediate attention, all at one time. Why don't nurses and doctors panic under pressure? They are both mentally prepared, well trained, and they practice triage. Schools are no different. Plan to train the staff and practice for a catastrophic event the same way you practice the fire drill.

Some examples of behavior that sends staff into spasms are the following:

- Barking orders only places those around you in a panic mode. Keep your voice at a determined level, not a shouting or screaming level.

- Pacing back and forth while trying to sort out what you need to do causes more confusion. Those around you are waiting for your direction.

- Racing off somewhere without getting all of the players at their assigned positions and tasks leaves everyone trying to remember what they are supposed to do. Stay put until you are sure the staff know what to do and begin doing it. If it does not put a staff member in harm's way, let someone else go to the scene until you get there.

- Don't forget the walkie-talkies. You don't have any at the school because you have never needed them? Get them.

 # What Should I Do and How Should I Do It?

Crisis

Examine Existing Documents and Procedures

By now, you have read the information the school uses. What areas of the document need adjusting, editing, or rewriting? Does every staff member know exactly what to do in a severe crisis? Do the recently hired teachers know what to do? When was the last documented day that practice occurred?

Assume that teachers are unsure of what to do in a catastrophic event. This is an area to discuss with staff during preplanning days before the students arrive. Because you are new to the school, no one will take issue if you decide to jump right in from day one to keep everyone safe. Start from the beginning.

When you walk around the school with the custodian, look at the traffic pattern for vehicles, buses, and students. This serves two purposes. First, you will begin to understand issues of general safety at your school. Second, this observation could provide you with information for your severe crisis response plan.

Ask several basic questions of those who have a history with the school. You will add your own questions.

- ◆ What is the established pattern for dismissal for buses, car riders, car drivers, bikers, and students who walk home?
- ◆ Is the established pattern for dismissal working? Why or why not?
- ◆ Does the system make sense to you?
- ◆ Are there adequate parking spaces for staff and students? If not, is there a plan in place to provide the needed space?
- ◆ Is there adequate parking when parents come to school for events, parent conferences, or parent meetings? How do parents know where to park?
- ◆ Is there an adjacent church or school that will allow overflow parking?

View the school's safety plan through the lens of a severe crisis. In your worst-case scenario, what would a severe Crisis Plan look like and under what conditions? If there is a Crisis Plan, does it address the events you imagine? Write your questions.

Create a Crisis Response Team

This is another group of people who are responsible for specific tasks during a crisis. Often, this team comprises those who are not responsible for a classroom of students. Office staff members usually are the core group, although you will need others. You will create a checklist for every member who is assigned a specific responsibility. The checklist should remain visible and easily accessible at all times. Everyone is cross-trained in case someone is absent on the day of the event.

Your Crisis Response Team can help to create the plan. At least you have a crisis response mind-set. There is no way to anticipate all of the possibilities. However, if you and your team recreate two or three of the worst things that can happen, other crises will be handled in a similar way.

Think of the possible situations that could occur based on your community and the experiences of other principals as you recall tragic events in schools over the last few years. Go through each of the possible scenarios from the perspective of the school community groups. Does everyone know what to do? How will they know? What method of communication do you plan for when events are unexpected? Where are the community resources you can access immediately?

- Will teachers know what to do?
- Will students know what to do?
- Will parents know what to do?
- Will the office staff know what to do?
- Will the support staff know what to do?
- Will bus drivers know what to do?
- Will visitors or substitute teachers know what to do?

Think of all the issues that must be addressed under the following real-life circumstances.

Scenario 1: Loose Criminal

A criminal is loose in the neighborhood, and the police have notified you that the school must not let anyone outside the classroom. The school must go into *lockdown* mode for an indefinite period of time. (Schools with an open campus have different issues to address than classrooms located in one building.) The problems are the following:

- Parents come to pick up their children during the day for doctor's appointments.
- Parents come to pick up their children at the end of the day.
- Parents will be waiting for their children to come home at the end of the day.
- Students must go outside the classroom to go to the cafeteria.
- Students are already in the cafeteria.
- Students are outside during physical education class or band practice.
- Students normally walk outside to get to their physical education class.
- Every class period requires students to come and go outside the building.
- Teachers, especially those newly hired, forget what lockdown really means and take their students across the campus to their assigned lunch time in the cafeteria.

- Teachers need an emergency lesson plan when keeping students for additional class time.
- The school gates remain open during school hours.

True Story

> It was after 9/11 during the anthrax alert. Police found a suspicious-looking package in a car located in a parking lot near the high school. The police required we lock down the school. Imagine holding 3,500 students for over two hours the last period of the day. It turned out to be an unfounded alarm. What a challenge.
>
> —High school principal

Scenario 2: Natural Disaster

A natural disaster is heading toward the school and all students must be dismissed immediately. The problems are the following:

- All students must contact their parents.
- Not all parents are available.
- All phone numbers are not current.
- The emergency file is not available for all teachers at the same time.
- All parents hear the news over the radio and drive to get their children.
- Parents arrive, park somewhere, and come crying into the office; most are hysterical. They want their children immediately.

Scenario 3: Missing Student

One of your students is missing. A kindergarten, middle school, or high school student reports to her teacher that another student started walking with her to school but then turned back home and wouldn't come with her, so she came to school by herself. She can't remember her friend's name or her grade. How will you find out who is missing? It's a school of 1,000 elementary students, 2,000 middle school students, or 3,500 high school students.

What steps would you follow to locate a missing student? Does your Crisis Plan provide you with everything you need to know and do? If not, what needs to be added?

You call the police. What do you ask them to do? The media gets the dispatch and immediately comes to your school, camera crews and all. Worse yet, it's a slow news day, and several television stations show up. The radio station announces that a child is missing from your school, but the school won't release the name. Word gets out to the parents. The child cannot be found?

Consider the following similar scenario with the same problem: In this case, the father of the missing child is finally contacted, only this time the missing student could have been the victim of custodial parent abduction. The problems are the following:

- Once the parent is involved, hysteria, emotional outbursts, and finger pointing occur.
- The parent calls his or her attorney, who may or may not show up asking for answers.
- The local media want immediate interviews with you.
- The local media want to interview the child's walking partner—now!
- The local media park outside the school waiting for students, parents, and teachers so that they can interview them.
- Your supervisor wants to be informed of any event that gives even the appearance of media coverage. However, the local media are at your doorstep before you can call anyone.

True Story

> It was bad enough that we couldn't find the child after school let out, but the hysteria of her parents and all of her relatives that came bursting into the lobby of the school was unbelievable. Come to find out the families had all been subjected to kidnappings in their native country. Trying to calm everyone down long enough for us to figure out where the child may have ended up was so hard, especially when we were dealing with a family who spoke limited English. Fortunately, a neighbor saw the child looking for her house and took her in until the neighbor could locate the parents. We were hours straightening this out. Every one of us was exhausted after that.
>
> —Elementary school principal

Scenario 4: School Shooting

A student brings a gun to school and begins shooting. Add all of the issues listed above to the additional ones below:

- The police arrive.
- The fire department arrives.

- ◆ Ambulances arrive.
- ◆ Parents arrive.
- ◆ The national media arrive by the end of the day.
- ◆ Onlookers arrive.
- ◆ Well-meaning "helpers" arrive.
- ◆ Parents, county office staff, and the media want an immediate list of all injured or involved students.
- ◆ A clean-up crew must be recruited, if necessary.

A crisis of this magnitude comes out of nowhere. You have no time to start reading a crisis manual. As the principal, you must know every possible response you must make without thinking. You can have a meltdown later, just not at the time. As you thought through every person's expectations and roles, did you consider the following issues that must be identified and organized, just in case—because the buck stops with you.

Television media become the most problematic issue that principals experience at a time of crisis.

- ◆ Is there someone at the district office whom you can call to get help with the media? If not, find someone. Television media are one group that takes on a life of its own. Handling insensitive news reporters is a principal's worse nightmare when you have to respond to the needs of your school community.
- ◆ Understand your responsibilities to the media based on the community. Ask your supervisor to clarify what you can and cannot do regarding the media.
- ◆ You may seek the advice of your supervisor about someone who can help you. Discuss the expectations up front. Prearrange procedures, protocol, and strategies so that his or her role as an outside support person is clear. How will you contact your helper?
- ◆ Do you have a "holding area" for the media? Who will help to monitor them—most national television media will not follow your requests to remain sensitive to the students, teachers, parents, or you. Is there a deputy sheriff available? Recruit one who can be on call to help you. Who is it? Is the phone number easily accessible?

Establish Communication Systems

Communication Inside the School

Communication with those inside the school must be discussed before a crisis. During a crisis, there is no time for an inservice on Crisis 101.

- Where are the phone numbers of every outside person with whom you will need immediate contact, such as county-level help?

- Under what circumstances will students be allowed to call home?

- Will you expect that if more than one child in the family attends the school, the oldest child will be the one to contact the parents?

- Have you identified the land lines available?

- Have you clarified how teacher's cell phones can be used? Will you let students use a teacher's cell phone?

- At the middle and high school levels, will students who have cell phones be allowed to use them? If so, will there be restrictions on whom they can call? (Reactive students may make a call to the media.)

- Have you identified a code system with the staff to alert them to various crisis responses? You say to the staff, for example, "I will announce over the intercom "Code Blue." That means there is a bomb threat. At that time, you will follow the fire drill plan and remain outside the building until given the signal to return." Perhaps your county already has a code system in place. In this way, you provide teachers with a way to know what is going on.

- Teachers, too, need a system to remember what to do under what circumstances. Some staff members may freeze under stress. Ask those teachers to identify themselves and find them a buddy to help get them unfrozen.

- Teachers need to understand that a crisis is a severe emergency and they must act—not react—and act immediately.

- Much like the code system, students need to understand that the teacher will have a way to get students' attention immediately and follow directions without question. A teacher might say, "If I say "Code Orange," that means that something serious has happened and I need your attention now. You will not ask questions; you will immediately do what you are told."

- If students must evacuate the building, what will you allow them to take with them?

- Is there a system in place to address a crisis that occurs when students are passing from class to class? How will they know what to do in the midst of all the noise and congestion?

- What system will you put in place to communicate the status of the event to the staff if they are unable to leave their classrooms?

- Spend time with staff discussing that when there is a crisis, communication with students should be in developmentally appropriate language. Students need information just as the teachers need it. Act, do not react. State the basic facts and follow the guidelines.

- Develop guidelines that define for teachers the conditions and circumstances under which television sets may be turned on for the express purpose of following a crisis. Some tragedies are so horrifying that students should not watch the event when it is happening.

- Reaction to a tragedy from some teachers is so dramatic that it affects instruction. Create guidelines to prevent this from happening. For example, you might say to the teachers, "In the event of a tragedy, do not automatically turn on the television set or discuss the crisis with the students. First, listen to your voice mail, check your e-mail, or wait for the intercom announcement (whatever process your school uses to communicate with everyone at one time). Directions will be provided at that time on how to proceed."

Parent Communication

- If everyone is driving to get their children at one time, how will they know where to park? Do you have signage that directs people to the holding area? Is that signage prepared ahead of time and stored in a known area? (This is no time to start running around looking for a marking pen and poster paper.)

- Will parents be informed ahead of time about where to park when the parking lot is full?

- If students call their parents, do they know what to say?

- What is the plan if the children can not reach their parents?

Communication with Emergency Services

- Is someone assigned to direct emergency crews to get through the traffic and parking lot and to the crisis site?

- Is there someone to give information about the student or students? Emergency crews need specific details—student identification, parent contact, emergency information—in case there is a need to transport to the hospital.

- Is there someone who knows the students to identify who is involved?
- Is there someone who can return to the office, get the needed information, and return to the emergency workers?

Who Is Responsible for Calling Which People?

You will not have time to make the mountain of phone calls that must be made almost simultaneously. You may need to contact the following people:

- County-level people: Superintendent and your supervisor—The principal makes these two calls only if time permits. Otherwise, this is assigned to someone else.
- All staff: Clarify exactly what everyone needs to know and do. This requires a focused staff meeting as early as preplanning days before school begins in the fall.
- A deputy sheriff to help manage traffic and possibly the media.
- Media response people to keep the media at bay until you are given directions by your supervisor about how and when to respond. Your supervisor may suggest someone, or you will find someone.

In addition, consider the following issues:

- Who will man the incoming calls? Will one land line be held for outgoing calls? Will outgoing calls occur with cell phones?
- Will there be an announcement on the answering machine that gives the current and updated information to parents for all incoming calls? In this way, the office staff is available for other urgent tasks.
- Each of the people you need outside the school must be contacted well in advance of any crisis, recruited "just in case," and placed on the roster of those to contact.

Who Will Assume the Logistical Tasks?

- Signs to direct parents to parking and to a "holding pen" such as the cafeteria
- Two-way radios and blow horns
- Coffee and water for the parents and emergency crews and placed in the holding area.

Following a crisis, there are many emotional concerns that cannot be ignored. It is important to understand that the aftermath of a crisis creates another layer of issues that must be addressed. For this, you need the guidance counselor to facilitate the next stage. This is the time when you and your assistant need to determine how to recoup from the trauma (Fein, 2003). You need a plan for *you* following a severe crisis.

True Story

We had just settled in for the school year when the hurricanes hit. Although I wanted to be home with my family, helping my wife take care of our damaged house, I had to supervise the school's community shelter. The Red Cross set up a place for those who could not stay in their homes. I told my own children that I had to be at my job instead of with them. It was so hectic; all the response workers had a thousand questions about the logistics in the school. I couldn't take a shower, and power was at a minimum. The first hurricane went for days. Finally, I could go home. I was there for two days, barely got some needed sleep, when the second hurricane hit. Back to school, same issues. Then, a third hurricane hit. I sent my wife and kids to stay with her parents and while they were gone, and I was manning the school shelter, my house was ransacked and robbed. Even my car was stolen. I didn't think it would ever end. I kept thinking, "Where is all this in my job description? How will we get school back on track? When will I get my life back together?" We eventually did, but it sure took a toll on everyone. Those are the stories I'll tell.

—High school assistant principal

Conflict

Once you think about handling a crisis, a conflict seems like small potatoes. Unfortunately, those in a conflict often act as if it were a crisis. It is all relative to the issues at hand and the frame of reference.

Conflict: Bandages

The most frequent reason that conflict occurs is the inability and unwillingness to confront a conflict head on. Different people handle conflict very differently.

Men may get frustrated or downright angry with another man and say what needs to be said, "man to man," so to speak. They then swat each other on the arm, move on to the next subject, and go watch football on the big screen somewhere. All is forgotten.

Conflict: Tissues

Other people become frustrated over some issue that they take personally, tell five of their friends, who tell five of their friends, and all 10 come to the aid and sympathy of the frustrated teacher. The person with whom there is a conflict is usually clueless about what the problem is, recognizes that he or she is being ignored, and now knows that "no one likes them."

Eventually, you, as the principal, may find out that two of your teachers are at odds with one another—probably over something that happened months ago, only now they make it public that they "don't like working together." At a time like this, the first impulse is to put the two together in a closed room and tell them to not come out until their issue is resolved. But that's what you do with third graders, and you can't imagine behavior among adults that would warrant the same resolution you would use with eight-year-olds. Yeah, right!

Instead, you practice your conflict-resolution skills that you learned in educational leadership classes and previous experiences to try to bring the problem to some reasonable solution. There are many strategies to assist people in resolving conflicts and books written on the subject. You read many of them and probably got As in those classes in college. However, in the real world, conflict is messier than those books might lead you to believe.

Often, the approach is based on your own style. It requires enormous patience to deal with two people who will tell you two completely different versions of the story that caused the conflict in the first place.

Consider the following interventions and questions to ask yourself and others.

- ◆ How did you find out? Did you find out from one of the two in conflict or from one of the 10 friends?
- ◆ Do you think the issue will blow over?
- ◆ If the two have had issues before, you may have to intervene.
- ◆ If so, start digging. When an issue explodes, there is almost always a much bigger issue underlying the problem. It's usually a family problem, significant other issue, or "life is getting in the way of their happiness."
- ◆ After speaking with each of them, bring them together and see whether you can help to bring resolution.

- Examine whether the conflict affects any other members of the staff. The conflict may occur among teachers, custodians, food service workers, paraprofessionals, or PTA members.
- Your level of involvement to help the two reach resolution depends on the severity of the issue. This is where you have to closely examine the time it will take and how much time you plan to spend on this issue.
- It's a time-management concern for a principal. Be careful about the amount of time you take to resolve conflicts between staff members.

Questions and Answers

Q: What should I do when I am appointed after the school year begins, and I don't have any time before students arrive to develop a severe Crisis Plan?

A: Determine when you can accomplish the task. The good news is that you have faster access to staff members who can help you with the plan. At least you can become mentally prepared as you think through the issues, even if they are not written down at the moment. This often can be accomplished while you are coming and going to school and during your think time. Because you will spend time in classrooms, you will develop the details during off-the-clock time when students are not in session and when you can get your Crisis Response Team to develop or modify the school's Crisis Plan. This should be a priority.

Q: I am new to the school. When a teacher comes to me with a problem, I don't know which issues are important and which are not.

A: Examine the issue. Is it school related? Ask three "why" questions. The teacher says, "I'm upset because …." You say, "Why?" The teacher responds, "Well, because…," and you say again, "Why?" After three why's, you'll get closer to the real issue.

You then say, "How do you plan to fix it?" "What do you want me to do?" "I'll give you the next five days to figure out what you plan to do, so come back and let me know what you did and how it is going."

Sometimes that works, and sometimes it doesn't. If, in five days, the staff member comes back and continues to whine, then you have two choices: If this is an ongoing feud and isn't being resolved, then a reality check for the staff members may be in order. You need to up the ante. You could say, "I am new, and I am committed to bringing together teams of people that can work together. I will recommend competent teachers who are also willing to help us reach our goal together. I am sure you will work this out so that we will have the teams we need." (In the back of your mind you are saying, "They better get over it, because I am tired of this. I'll keep my eyes and ears open, whether or not they are good teachers. I will start the documentation to let them go at the end of the year—if I have to.")

You then give each of them a dated letter or memo within three days, thanking them for discussing the issues that were raised. You are certain that the conflict that occurred will be resolved and that they will be a contributing member of the school team. They get the letter, because you deliver it, and you have the beginning of documentation if you need it. By doing this, (1) attention is called to a conflict between the two; (2) you go on notice that the conflict will be resolved; and (3) you have the beginning of the documentation that you will file.

Word will spread quickly that you are not unreasonable (after all, you put the responsibility for resolution back on their shoulders) and that you are committed to building a school in which teachers work together. This is smart. The first memo you write will have everyone buzzing.

If this is a bandage on an open wound, then continue to keep your ears open. Get into their classrooms to see whether there is a bigger issue. If you are at all suspicious that something isn't as it should be, call your supervisor in charge of nonreappointment of staff and get advice on how to proceed. You will need every bit of documentation possible. Most of it you won't use. But, if you need it, it is there.

Q: Some teachers are at my door all the time with a new problem. How can I deal with them politely?

A: Is there anyone who can give you a history of the staff member in question, such as your mentor, assistant, or secretary? From your current perspective, are the issues considered serious or not? Is each issue different, and he or she is just whining for the sake of getting your attention? Is he or she just a pain in the neck?

Some teachers are more high maintenance than others. Who knows why? Ask them to send you an e-mail message or put their concerns or issues in writing "so that you will have time to think about their concerns and get back to them." You can hope that teachers won't want to take that kind of time and will eventually decide to fix the problem themselves.

There is a response to continuous nagging. Say to the teacher, "Explain what you want me to do" and "What can you do to solve your problem?"

Q: The Faculty Committee can be very aggressive. How do I know whom they really represent?

A: Groups of teachers often form in schools under the guise of "staff representatives" who help to communicate the needs of the staff to the principal. They have different names for the group depending on the school district. Often, they are the union representatives. Frequently, they refer to the collective "we" when really they speak only for a few. How do you know? You don't. However, here is one strategy to try: Ask the group to provide you with their questions before the meeting with them. This gives you time to think about ways to respond and do some background checking on the issue. Then, you meet. You address their questions and explain the situation. Someone is taking notes, and so are you.

When the meeting is over, you receive the recording secretary's notes, combine them with yours, and send them back to the faculty representatives for editing. Make sure the turnaround time is quick, no more than three days. Then, respond to everyone on the entire staff through e-mail, voice mail, or hard copy. A question-and-answer format works well. In this case, everyone knows the issues you heard and everyone knows how you responded. Again, minutes go to every staff member, including all noninstructional staff.

You will be surprised at how often a question comes up with the faculty group that makes you think the entire world is mad at you for something you should have done, when in reality, it only reflects the views of a very few. Watch the number of teachers who, upon reading your response, say, "I don't feel that way" or "I don't know how you heard that."

The collective "we" or the collective "they" must be nailed down. Who are "we" and who are "they?" How many are you talking about? In this way, you can quickly sort out and develop a plan for the serious issues compared to the frivolous, self-serving ones.

 **Survival Tips**

Train every staff member to respond to a Crisis Plan. Provide adequate training in the plan so that every staff member knows exactly what to do and under what circumstances. The Crisis Plan can be located in a colored binder and placed on a shelf or plastic holder near every classroom exit door. This provides easy access and clear identification.

Create evacuation maps. All exit signs for each situation and for each room illustrate room evacuation procedures. These are posted by all exit doors. If they already exist, are they current? As schools add classrooms, evacuation paths may change.

Management issues are easier to handle at the beginning of your assignment. Concentrate on those dealing with health and safety. It's an important part of your early responsibilities. Staff members are usually willing to adjust to issues of safety and health, even if your ideas are different from your predecessor. Don't make hasty decisions, unless it could be life threatening. However, decisiveness is good.

Carefully determine issues that might reach the level of a conflict and those that are simply issues to resolve. Because you are new, you need to do your homework before making that distinction. Don't assume that an issue is so simple that a resolution will come quickly. To make you feel better, ask your principal friends to share experiences in which something so simple on the surface is really a big deal to some members of the staff. Ask them how they resolved the issue.

Decide what you will say to the media, especially during a catastrophic event.

- You don't have to say anything right away. If you need time to respond, say so.
- Do not let a reporter pressure you into responding before you are ready. The reporter may have a deadline, but you don't.
- You can say "I am unable to speculate on that, but we are very concerned about…"
- If you don't know the answer to a question, say so.
- Direct the reporter to someone else in the district who can respond. (District-level people are there to help. You have already contacted them as part of your Crisis Plan—take advantage of their expertise.)
- Never go off the record. Your reality off the record is not always the reporter's.
- Recognize that remarks made off the cuff' make the best headlines for the reporter. Be careful.

Avoid unnecessary conflict. Conflict happens even when you have the best intention to minimize it. This is one way that causes a conflict to get worse. Assume for the sake of discussion that you believe "I am who I am, and I'll take care of any situation the way I usually do because that's what I do."

If you are gifted in the art of handling all people the same way, under every circumstance, with never a misunderstanding, you must bottle this gift and sell it. Otherwise, you need a serious attitude adjustment if you plan on living long in this job.

Your administrative life revolves around applying your leadership skills, which change with every situation—especially when you are new to the school. Step back, evaluate, develop a plan, and then approach the conflict. In the meantime, listen, take notes, bite your tongue, and wait for another day to help resolve the problem. Little can be accomplished if you allow a reactive response during the heat of the moment to cloud your otherwise logical approach to problem solving.

Summary

Principals face the fact that a severe crisis may occur in any school setting. That school could be yours. In the last few years, principals have lived through the most unfathomable part of the job, life-and-death events. This chapter provided principals with food for thought regarding what to do, what to think about, and how to plan for the worst that could happen.

If you are lucky, you may live through an entire career and never experience a catastrophic event, but an administrator must be prepared. You never know. Talk to or read about those principals who have lived through it if you have any doubt that it could happen in any school, in any town, or in any city.

Appropriate responses to a severe crisis are based on communication, crowd control, media reaction, and following a proactive plan. Your responsibilities include the following:

- Keep your head while everyone about you may be losing theirs.
- Model the calm and controlled strength that leaders demonstrate.
- Remain patient and sensitive.

Everyone will look to you for guidance—so, guide.

Common conflicts usually do not affect the entire school community but occur between one or more people within the staff. The degree of the disruption depends on the principal or assistant principal's ability to help those in conflict solve their way to a satisfactory solution that is mutually agreed upon.

This chapter also pointed out something that is well known to all—women and men handle conflict in very different ways. Recognize and respond to the difference.

A principal must consciously determine the amount of time that conflict takes from his or her day. Once a principal knows the staff better, it becomes easier to know whom to respond to and to what degree. Until the staff knows the principal better, those who are high maintenance can pull the energy right out of you unless you are careful.

On the other hand, a new principal may spend very little time trying to resolve a conflict, only to discover that a serious problem developed because of lack of attention to the matter. It's a tightrope, one that principals face every moment. You must remain insightful and sensitive—and very in tune with the staff.

Reflections

1. Discuss your personal behaviors during a crisis. How would those behaviors help or hinder a triage situation?

2. Imagine your current school. As you examine your campus, what potential crisis could occur for which there is no existing plan for response? What plan would you put into place? Describe the situation and your plan to fix it. Explain how you would communicate your plan to the staff.

3. Have your colleagues examine your school's Crisis Plan. Can you follow it? Is anything missing? If so, what? How would you propose solving the problem? Create a plan to address the specific crisis response issues that appear to be missing from your current school plan.

4. Create a scenario in which there is an ongoing conflict that affects your entire team. What is the problem? How would you go about resolving the issue?

5

Getting and Keeping Organized: Working Smarter, Not Harder

(As Soon as You Are Appointed)

Time is your most valuable commodity. There is rarely enough of it. Some time is under your control, and some time is imposed on you. How can you organize and manage as much as possible?

Controlling your time requires discipline and a methodical look at every strategy possible to do your job efficiently. You are entering a new job in which everything is new, so you may as well add "getting organized" to the list so that you can work smarter, not harder.

On the other hand, you may be one of those highly organized, enormously efficient people who always knows where every scrap of paper is located, has every file exactly where you can find it, and has a mind like a steel trap. If that is the case, skip this chapter.

If you are like most mortal principals, information comes at you fast and furiously while you are multitasking, carrying on multiple conversations at once, and making several decisions every hour. All the while, you are receiving e-mails, voice mail messages, papers, phone calls, and a beeping calendar reminder from the latest piece of technology. If that is the case, there may be some ideas in this chapter that will help.

When Do I Begin?

There are four time frames:

1. As soon as you receive your appointment
2. As soon as you move into your office
3. As soon as you acknowledge that first "to do" item
4. As soon as you recognize the existing system needs revamping

What Should I Do and How Should I Do It?

Organize Your *New* Office and the *Old* Stuff

Organizing your "stuff" should not require sorting through all of your predecessor's treasures just in case you might need it. What can go from your predecessor's treasure of papers, binders, and e-mails?

*   Ask your predecessor to take almost everything out of his or her office. Let him or her know that you will ask for copies of memos from the author if someone asks for something you don't have. In this age when rules and regulations change constantly, only the most recent information is necessary.

*   Often, your predecessor will empty the file folders but leave you the labeled files. Send the old file folders to the recycling bin. Start over with your own system.

*   Old manuals from the district or training that your predecessor attended need to go to "manual heaven."

What should stay from your predecessor's stuff?

*   Memos and e-mails from the last six months. If you need current information, call the author of the memo for a new copy.

*   Monthly files (sometimes referred to as "tickler files") are files labeled for each month (Davenport, 2001) and contain the important events and details surrounding last year's calendar. The monthly

files identify each of the tasks and district requirements, which never change from year to year.

- January file: Forms for the School Improvement Plan, because this is the time of year when that process usually begins. You can read what to expect.
- May file: Graduation ceremony details
- June/July file: Forms to complete from the results of standardized testing. (These will undoubtedly change by the time the new scores arrive, but it will give you a frame of reference for what you can anticipate).

- Files of teachers who have remained at the school, including assessments.
- Binders with information that someone thinks you should keep (or should you?). You may decide that binders filled with procedural things are best housed with the head of that department or with your secretary. Then, you can always go to him or her if and when you need the information and learn the procedures of the department. Topics might include food service, guidance, custodial, exceptional education, facilities, and second-language learners.

Organize Your *Old* Stuff from Your *Old* Office

Whether you are a former teacher, coach, or guidance counselor, you have very little you can use in your new life that can't be retrieved from the boxes you've taken to your garage. If you are an assistant principal who is about to assume a principal's life, only a few things are reusable unless you are replacing the principal in your existing school.

This is a time to clear out all of your old things. If you are the type who cannot part with anything, box it up, label it well, and keep it at home. Store those textbooks from college and educational leadership classes. Of course, you paid a bundle for all of them, but the chances of using them as a reference while you are on the clock is minimal. At the very most, you may unearth your favorite references on the weekend when you are desperate for an idea. This usually happens at home and therefore off the clock.

If you were in a strong apprentice program, you are lucky, and there may be pearls of wisdom that you need. This is especially true if your appointment is in the same school district. Keep as much as possible in the garage, and take what you need to your new office only *when* you need it, not *if* you need it.

If you feel that you waste time rummaging through papers to find what you need, lose information, or generally feel disorganized, now is the time to turn over a new leaf. Begin organizing from scratch and learn lessons from the past. Remember the stories of your great-grandparents about the Depression? They are no longer relevant. It is not necessary to squirrel away multiple items or copies just in case they will be scarce some time.

Organize Your *New* Stuff and Your *New* Office

Before you move one picture onto your new desk, make sure all of your predecessor's things are completely removed. Take everything home first. (It may be convenient to move all of your boxes from your former life to your new one in one move, but it is not a good idea.) It's too easy to move unnecessary things.

In addition, it gives the wrong impression to leave boxes stacked outside your predecessor's office waiting for him or her to move out. You won't want to give the appearance that you are pushing the "old guy or gal" out. Wait to move into a clear and clean office. Box up one box containing your family picture and the first few things you want to put into your office, leave it in your car, and wait until the appropriate time to begin setting up.

Your New Office Environment

Of course you are anxious to move in. However, once your assignment begins, the time to create your working environment will be limited. Too many other things will become more important.

Take advantage of being new. Ask the district to paint your office before you move in. In some cases, principals paint their new offices themselves. It's motivating when the room looks as new as possible. A few cosmetic changes are a subtle way to let everyone know that a new person has arrived. (Think light green. This is a soothing color.) If your desk "came over on the arc," then your supervisor may even help you spring for a new desk. Or can you find the money in your budget somewhere?

Whatever it takes, create a comfortable, inviting, and professional appearance—think it through. View your office not only from the perspective of the way you want it but from the perspective of the students, teachers, parents, and your supervisor.

What specific visuals do you want staff, faculty, students, and parents to see as soon as they sit down for a conference in your office? What should you place on your "wall of fame?" Where is it located? Sit down in the chair or chairs where teachers, students, and parents will sit when talking to you. What will be in their line of vision?

The Rules of Organization

Use it daily? Place it within hand's reach.

Use it weekly? Place it within arm's reach (without leaving the chair).

Use it monthly? Place it somewhere in your office.

Use it less than once a month? Place it somewhere outside your office.

Your Desktop

The Shape of Your Desk

- If you have enough floor space, the most effective desk configuration is a U shape. This allows your computer to sit at the base of the U, with one side assigned to your personal work space and the other side to hold meetings with one or two people.

- If you cannot use a U shape, then an L shape is the next-best configuration. The computer is placed at the corner, and you still have one area for your personal work space and the other area for meetings (Davenport, 2001).

The Work Area on Top of Your Desk

- Devoting one side of your desk to personal work space provides a way to answer the phone, sign papers, and complete tasks that require a quick turnaround. In this way, when you are interrupted for the bazillionth time, your task remains intact and won't become buried under the other tasks that accompany the interrupter.

- The idea is to create three distinct and specific areas: One for work, one for your computer, and one for meetings.

The Work Tools on Top of Your Desk

- Keep a phone log with carbonless paper. In this way, if you must delegate the message, tear off the message and keep a record of the call and, if needed, the person delegated.

- Keep only those items that you use constantly. If there is a desk drawer, then most every tool belongs there. The clearer the desk surface, the more efficiently you will work.

- Replace paper clips with staples or binder clips. Paper clips fall off.

- Replace your old college cup filled with miscellaneous pens, pencils, and markers with one pencil and one pen. Keep all the reserves in your desk drawer. If your predecessor felt that you should have all of the tools left over from his or her old stuff, get rid of them. You deserve new stuff.

The Organizational Piece above or near Your Desk

- There are a few documents that you use every day, including such things as: teachers' schedules; teachers' names; room numbers; phone extension numbers; e-mail addresses; the monthly calendar; school map and room numbers; district-level phone numbers; and any additional documents you consistently need at your fingertips.

- For easy access, some office catalogues contain an organizer that looks such as a notebook binder on a metal jointed arm. It holds solid plastic sleeves to insert any frequently used information. It is attached to the edge of your desk and functions best right above your phone. This organizer does not take up desk space. Otherwise, you will need a small binder that contains the same documents within arm's reach.

The Organizational Pieces on Top of Your Desk

- Use three stack trays (Davenport, 2001): "in," "pending," and "to read." These go on the personal work space area of your desk.

- Develop a system with your secretary to help you keep the categories organized. Your secretary can receive your mail, sort it out, highlight a date for action (if one is part of the document), and place items in their designated trays.

- In tray: This tray contains all of the new things you get in and out in one day. It keeps all of the things you need to respond to today. This is where your phone messages, written requests from the staff, documents to sign, etc., go. This is the one box that is cleaned out every day before you go home. Everything taken out of this box has a home, even if the home is the trash can. Each person who has access to this box must know what goes in it.

  A memo might require only the recording of the time, place, and date of a meeting you must attend. Record what you need and throw away the memo.

- Pending tray: Items in this tray contain a *date that requires your action*—it might be a meeting to attend or a report due.

A report due, with the date and accompanying forms to complete, require that you record the date due and a reminder at least two to three weeks in advance of the deadline on your portable calendar. The report forms can go into the pending file until you need them.

◆ To Read tray: First, include must-know information, such as memos, documents, faxes, and e-mails with no date attached. These should be cleaned out by the end of the week. This is information that you will read between meetings, at the end of the day, while listening to a ranting and raving parent on the phone, or while waiting before some appointment or event.

If you haven't cleared out this tray by the end of the week, put the contents in your briefcase, tote bag, or file folder that you place in your project box under your desk to take home and read during television commercials.

Second, include magazines and professional literature. These do not need a separate tray because it is rare that you will have time to read these during the work week.

- As soon as you go through your weekly To Read tray, the literature can be moved out of the tray.

- Place magazines and professional journals in your briefcase or tote bag to read over the weekend. In that way, you can concentrate on the information and pay specific attention to your need-to-know articles.

- Some articles are so profound that you will mark them with a note to copy; do that first thing when you get to the office on Monday, file it immediately (probably in a file labeled "research"). Make sure the important information concerning the source is written on the article page (journal, volume, number, date, and pages).

- Other articles are important to your need-to-know information. You will mark the text with something such as a sticky note that acts as a tab, with the topic labeled and clearly identified without going through the entire magazine to locate the information later.

- Another way to identify important articles is to label the article topic and page number on the outside of the magazine.

- Cardboard magazine holders work well to store the magazines. Each subscription should have its own holder, filed by date. Because most reading of professional journals and magazines occurs at home, it makes sense to leave the magazine files at home.

- Sunday night, every item in your tote bag or briefcase should be filed in your magazine holder, identified as "to copy" or "must file at work." Everything else can be thrown away. (Stay out of the "I didn't get to it" trap and take the same papers and magazines back and forth every day. It is not efficient. You eventually will have to make a decision. Practice your decisive skills). Do something with that pesky paper by Sunday night every week.

One Calendar, Three Parts

Your calendar is among the most important tools you own. One thing is clear: You must operate out of only one very portable calendar, all of the time (Eisenberg & Kelly, 1997). You have entered a world in which a calendar drives most of your life and, by now, in your adventure through administration, you realize the importance of keeping track of just about everything.

Electronic calendars become more sophisticated every time you turn around and continue to take on new names. Whatever brand or style you use, it must be extremely portable. The calendar on your desk computer, although highly functional, is not portable. It is awkward for many and time-consuming to access compared to other methods. Choose the one that works for you and that will conveniently handle all the scheduling and note-taking capabilities you need.

Don't worry if you prefer the old-fashioned pencil-and-paper calendar. Just make sure you record in pencil because times and dates change frequently. Choose a portable size that you can access quickly and easily.

Your calendar should contain three basic parts:

1. A 12-month calendar with enough writing space to record the year's dates and appointments for events, observations, when you must start a project or report, when the same project or report is due, when something is due from someone else, your follow-up dates, and meetings.

2. A to-do list so that you can record details of activities for each day and phone calls to make and return (Hemphill, 2002).

3. A place for related notes, such as invitations, maps to other schools, and important phone numbers.

Dates

12-Month Calendar

Regardless of the type of organizer you use—paper or electronic—your calendar should always be within hand's reach, wherever you locate. There is common agreement about the key pieces of information that must be available to you at all times and in one place. Before your assignment begins, you can enter nonnegotiable dates.

In Chapter 1, you entered the *first round* of dates—those that the district imposes. This would include dates for the standardized tests, school holidays, and any days that students are not in school.

This serves two purposes. First, it starts you thinking about how efficient your schedule must become. Second, this calendar will demonstrate the number of instructional days lost because of holidays and events. You will identify the additional times and days lost based on the next series of dates you enter on your major calendar, nonnegotiable school dates that take up instructional time. The purpose is to focus on the instructional time available for the students (see Chapter 8).

In large schools, several additional calendars of schedules exist, such as athletic events, facility rental, master schedule, performing arts, and special events. You need a plan to determine which events you must attend. If you have an assistant, this also helps you begin planning which people will be responsible for which activities and events. These assignments also should be noted on your calendar.

The *second round* of entries reflects your supervisor's requirements, such as management meetings, district committee meetings, and meetings with your supervisor.

The *third round* of entries includes dates that were already scheduled by your predecessor and cannot change. These are school-specific dates and include parent meetings, events, and activities already scheduled for the year that are not negotiable.

The *fourth round* of entries includes dates that you know will become your responsibility, such as dates for formal teacher observations, individual meetings with teachers (described in Chapter 2), inservice training at the school and district levels, and dates when final teacher assessments are due.

The *fifth round* of entries requires conscientious transfer of home information to your portable calendar. For example, you know you will be in trouble with your spouse if you forget to pick up your child from day care on Thursday, January 12th, at 5:00 p.m. or with your supervisor if you forget a meeting with the fire inspector at your school at the same time.

Day-to-day schedules should be recorded continuously and range everywhere from a date on which you expect a teacher to hand in a report, to dates you record for the school newsletter, to meetings you arrange.

To-Do List

During your early morning time, review your calendar and create a "to do today" list. A priority list becomes unusable as soon as teachers arrive, parents, and students need you. They don't read your to-do list. Number one on your list should be a meeting with your secretary to coordinate your calendars and discuss any immediate issues for the day (before the teachers arrive).

Don't attempt to make a list of everything you would like to do during the day; rather, what are the immediate tasks? For example, during observation time, your to-do list would include a schedule of teacher observations and conferences.

True Story

I have a 30-minute drive to get to work. I keep my calendar with my to-do list on the seat beside me. So, when I am stopped at a red light I can glance over, read my calendar for the day, and start thinking about my priorities.

When I get to school, I have already planned what I need to do. If I haven't already written my list, I do it first thing, after I get my coffee brewing. I know I'll be lucky to get the first thing done on my list. But I'll have organized my thoughts and gained my focus. Between my coffee, my mental preparation, and my completed to-do list, I am ready with positive energy to get the day going.

—Elementary school principal

Important Phone Numbers

Record important phone numbers in your cell phone, electronic hand-held device, rolodex, or on your paper-and-pencil portable calendar. Important school-related numbers and personal phone numbers require easy access.

Telephone Log

Create a form (pages are often in a small binder) that states the date, time, person, and nature of the call. This important method of keeping track of what you said and to whom is valuable documentation.

Date	Time	Person	Nature of the Call

The binder is kept by the phone for convenience. If follow-up dates are required, such as a parent conference, you will transfer that date to your portable calendar. Recording adequate information is another reference when communicating any pertinent details when another person, such as a teacher, needs the details from the phone or voice mail conversation.

Inside Your Desk (At Arm's Reach)

- ◆ The monthly files (tickler file) described earlier
- ◆ Budget categories
- ◆ "At-risk" staff member files

  The hanging file tab may say something innocuous such as "work in progress" (for confidentiality's sake), but each folder contains information and paperwork on each teacher who requires special attention. It may be a teacher who is on an improvement plan that began with your predecessor or a teacher you identify as needing specific documentation to support your concerns. (Don't forget to record follow-up meetings on your calendar.)

- ◆ Make additional files *when* you need them, not *if* you might need one.

Under Your Desk: Project File

These files are more easily placed in a portable file, the kind that often has wheels so that it can conveniently travel home with you (because you need uninterrupted time). It will hold hanging files. Office supply and hardware stores have a variety of options that are small but functional. Files on wheels are easier to access than a briefcase or tote bag because you don't have to keep opening, pulling files out, and sorting through them before you can begin. Just grab the lever and go.

On nights that you work, between meetings or after school, the project file is more conveniently obtained. It stays off your work space because you rarely work on it during the day. It is out of sight, but not out of mind (if you look at the floor at all, it keeps staring at you, reminding you it needs attention).

The computer printer conveniently stores under the desk unless there is another location that is within arms reach. If a credenza or countertop is within arm's reach, that is another option. Use the rule that you shouldn't get out of your chair to go to the printer—it is not efficient.

Stack trays work well with a tray for copy paper: one for letterhead paper, another for fax sheets.

Your Office Cupboard

There are documents and information that are important, yet typically you need the files only during specific times of the year. Supplies are also in your office that help you obtain what you need quickly. These items can be stored on shelves in a cupboard.

Binders

A small new binder for information referenced frequently is often easier to use when it is self-contained because it contains text-heavy sections and therefore is too bulky for a file folder. Store these on a shelf or cupboard. Ask the author of the binder for a new one. You want only up-to-date information available. Label the contents on the spine for easy recognition on a shelf in your office. Make sure the subcategories are accurately labeled with a tab.

- The *human relations* binder contains all of the information needed for teacher observations, documented examples, and any other information your district provides. *Memorize this information.*

- *Instructional and noninstructional contract* binders provide all of the supporting information that surrounds the procedures outlined in your human relations binder. Contracts for both instructional and noninstructional staff require easy access; therefore, make a new binder for each group. Also *memorize this information;* it will keep you out of a heap of trouble.

- The *Crisis Plan* binder is the one you developed in Chapter 4 and provided staff and office with copies. A colored binder identifies this information faster. *Memorize this information.* You rarely have time to read this during a real crisis.

- *Standardized test scores* may end up in more than one binder. Label the spine of each binder to accurately reflect the contents.

- A *parent organization* binder holds information on the last two years—so you have some history.

- A *School Improvement Plan* binder holds information on the last two years.

- A *School Advisory Council* binder holds information on the last two years.

- Keep *staff files* on all staff members who remain at the school but are not considered at risk.

    You will be unfamiliar with the staff members and need quick access to these files. They need to stay in your office. In large schools, you will find, create, or purchase a place to house these records.

Options include a locking office filing cabinet or a locking file cabinet on wheels. The file will also contain hanging files with the blank forms needed for each phase of the assessment process and individual yearly teacher development plans. Create separate groupings for instructional from noninstructional staff members.

Personal Emergency Kit

- Grooming and survival: Every principal needs a survival kit that contains the essentials for attending late-night or district-level meetings, such as toothbrush and toothpaste. For the times when you experience "one of those days," you'll probably add aspirin and antacids.
- Nutritional food: Create a box of nonperishable nutritional food such as energy bars, raisins, and dried fruit. Sometimes you'll need to grab something to eat on the run. Your personal emergency kit can store easily in a box on your cupboard shelf.

Extra Office Supplies

- Computer toner kept in reserve saves time. When you are in the middle of a project and your computer runs out of toner, it is frustrating to run around finding a new cartridge.
- The typical paper, staples, pens, ruler, etc., store easily in the cupboard and need not take up office drawer space.

Questions and Answers

Q: How can I make a filing system look professional?

A: Arrange with your secretary to make the categories for you so that they will remain consistently labeled (with the same style label) and easier to find. Your quickly scrawled label won't hold the test of time for efficient access. Start your system with new hanging files and new file folders. Recycle the old ones.

- Hanging files organize the big topics.
- File folders hold the subtopics.
- If you are using color-coded file folder labels, place the colored strip on the bottom so that the text is closer to the top and easier to read.
- Place the file label in alternate patterns to make the topics easier to find.

- Think carefully about how you will label the file so that you remember where to find what you are looking for.

Q: I am stopped everywhere on campus with a thousand questions from the faculty, and I make instant decisions. Some conversations end up setting a date to do something. How do I keep track of that information?

A: You have a few options:

- Discuss whatever you wish, but make it clear to the staff member that you need a written note with the dates you just made so that you can confirm the time (then you can coordinate with your calendar).

- Tell the staff member to e-mail their request to you (if there is that capability in your school). Then, you can record the date and purpose on your portable calendar and file the e-mail.

- Make it clear to staff that if they expect you to make a decision about anything, they must do it when and where you can give them your undivided attention, take notes, and keep track of the discussion. In large schools, have staff set up a time to meet with you when both of you are sitting down.

- Carry a small notepad or pile of sticky notes in a shirt, jacket, skirt pocket, or identification holder (described below) to record commitments for dates, times, teacher, and purpose. The trick is to instantly record the information when you return to your office (otherwise, you will forget and the notes end up in the washing machine).

- Passport holders sold for airline convenience and worn around the neck with a place for an identification picture work well. There is a place for notes. If your school requires identification pictures anyway, it serves multiple purposes.

True Story

I left my office and by the time I got to the Media Center, I must have made 15 decisions. People stop me every few feet to ask me a question about something where I need to give an answer. Keeping track of what I said is really hard in a school this size, especially when I may not get back to my office for a couple of hours or so.

—High school principal

Q: I must get 100 e-mails a day, and you can imagine what happens if I am out of the school for even one day. Then I have a bunch of voice mail messages. How do I keep all of these messages organized?

A: Treat e-mail and voice mail messages the same way you treat hard-copy memos.

- If the message contains a date for which you are responsible, record the date on your portable calendar and delete the message. (If you should not have deleted it, it is retrievable from the computer file).

- If there is more pertinent information that you must know, make a copy as well. Depending on the urgency of the date, the copy could go in your Pending tray on top of your desk or in your monthly file.

- If someone else can act on the message, record the pertinent date on your calendar, forward the message, and delete it.

- Use a three-line rule for e-mails from staff. For example, one high school principal with 3,000 students has a rule, "Whatever you need to say, say it in three lines. That is all I have time to read."

Q: Why a telephone log?

A: The telephone log works best when someone calls you with a concern or something you need to do. Conversely, when you call someone, particularly a parent, make notes about the conversation. A log provides you with enough space to create the details needed so that you have important documentation that the call occurred, the date, and the nature of the call.

- Parents with selective memory loss could call your boss with the typical "The principal never returns my calls." The log provides more room for writing detailed information so that when you respond to your boss, the parent, or whomever, you have specific details to verify the communication.

- If a parent calls and complains about a teacher, contact the teacher as soon as possible. Taking careful notes on your log provides an efficient system (because you will find your notes in the telephone log binder and not lose them). In this way, when you communicate with the teacher, the details are not forgotten.

- Often, you will call a district-level person with questions or a maintenance supervisor with a request for help. Noting the call reminds you of when you called and the purpose. It, too, provides documentation so that you can respond, "I called you on the following dates with the same request."

Q: How do I organize all of the testing data?

A: Investigate the level of support from the school district. You need several types of data: whole school, individual student scores, student scores from individual teachers, item analysis, and comparative data over the last two years.

The school should already possess some available data. It may not be organized in a way that makes sense to you. In this case, as you analyze the information, develop a system (usually in binders) with clearly identified topics (using tabs).

Often, the district-level computer system is not sophisticated enough to analyze individual or group scores by teacher or within subcategories that you think important. If you need more information, start by requesting the information you need from the country level and from a principal who is particularly good at analyzing data. It is easier to ask for help than to try to seek out a system on your own. Then, you can analyze the data according to your needs.

 ## Survival Tips

One system is the hardest to maintain—follow-through on issues, concerns, and staff member's requests. Conscientiously keep track. Create a system so that you will follow up on any issue that is brought to your attention.

You want to have coffee and water available, for yourself and guests, and a place to keep your lunch, but the cafeteria is located away from your office area. You're making more money now. Invest in a small refrigerator, a microwave to place on top of it, and a coffee pot (if you need one). Whatever you need that saves time. Create an unobtrusive place for your home-away-from-home appliances.

Official guests come to your school from time to time. Wear your public relations hat. Purchase a set of real dishes and silverware. (Perhaps your parent organization will help out, or you can find discretionary money somewhere.) This provides a professional image when hosting community members, your supervisor, or county-level staff. Paper plates, cups, and plastic utensils give a different image.

Your secretary can help you create the welcome that is important. On occasions when a group visits your school, the food service staff can help you out with goodies.

When moving from your former office or classroom, avoid packing and removing your "wall of fame" and personal items during the time students and teachers are present. You are leaving, and your friends and students will be less upset if they don't see your identity slowly moving away. Wait until a weekend to move visible things. In the meantime, clean out your files, box, and label them. Take them home as soon as possible.

Conversely, wait until your predecessor has completely moved out before you move in. Take your boxes home first, and bring them to your new office only *when* you need them, not *if* you need them.

You must have quiet time to get ready for your day. Learn to become a morning person and start work at least 30 minutes before you know people will need you. Otherwise, you need time at the end of the day to get ready for the next day.

- Arrive early or stay late to create your to-do list and to clear out your desktop trays.
- You must be ready to set a positive, upbeat image for all staff members as soon as they come to work. So you are not a morning person—no one wants to begin a work day with a crabby boss, so smile anyway.
- Model the expectations you have for staff members—be prepared for the class before the students come.

Summary

Creating and maintaining a highly organized system will be an important life saver on the job. Without such a plan, you waste valuable time, frustrating those around you who must accommodate your lack of organization and wasting their time.

The amount of information that comes to you can be staggering. Never in your educational career will you be responsible for so much for so many. Each suggestion in this chapter provided you with ideas to use or ways to assess a system that will be convenient and efficient for you.

This is an opportunity to organize everything you need at your fingertips, within arm's reach, in your office, and near your office. Everything will have a place that you establish.

A common reaction to all of the information your predecessor tells you about or shows you is to keep it, then take out what you don't need later. Well, later rarely happens because once the teachers come, your time will be spent in ways other than sorting through your predecessor's old stuff.

The recommendation: (1) Start from scratch, retaining only a few essential pieces of information. Put the saved papers in new file folders with new labels, and place the insides of essential binders into new ones with labels on the spine. You and your secretary can organize a system that you understand, that makes sense, and that you can efficiently maintain. (2) Use a portable calendar to record dates that are your responsibility, including follow-up dates. This calendar should be with you at all times and will become your personal and professional lifeline. This is smart and efficient.

Organize your day to manage as much of your time as possible. This organizational system provides immediate and efficient access to the multiple pieces of information that come your way every day.

In this way, you will become recognized as a principal who does what you say you will do, when you say you will do it. You keep track of other's deadlines so that you take a continuous pulse on each person for whom you are responsible. In short, you can be counted on.

Reflections

1. Describe the areas of your office that are well organized. Describe the areas of your office where you have difficulty finding what you need when you need it.

2. Create an efficient system. Draw a sketch of your office area and where you would place your organizers. Reorganize areas that create problems. Pay attention to items in your office you have not looked at in a year. Describe the items that you can get rid of. If not, why not?

3. Create a telephone log that works for you. The purpose is to create a system of documentation for calls made and received.

4. Describe ways to organize and respond to voice mail and e-mail.

5. Describe your organizational system to keep track of teacher requests, meetings you must attend, and dates for accomplishing tasks you assign to others. How will you keep track of tasks that require you to follow up on issues that are generated in conversations and conferences?

6

Understanding and Establishing Positive Relationships: Building Trust—I Was a Teacher Once, but Who Are These People?

(First Two Months on the Job)

Building trust is a complex process when you are working with large groups of people. Think of your position as a new principal in the following way:

One day the director of the school and family projects arrives at your door announcing that you will now have a new second home.

"Come with me," she says.

You think, "Wow! A new second home—cool."

She continues, "By the way, you will also have a new family. (Count the number of staff for whom you will be responsible—50, for example.) We must give you all 50 of your adopted children at one time. They come from different backgrounds and experiences. There is a broad range of ages. They will live with you under the same roof at the same time."

"Hello, Dad or Mom," the 50 yell at one time.

All 50 children become yours overnight. The 50 children expect you to pay attention to each one, neglecting no one. Every component of your family dynamics comes into play. With one major difference, you've never had so many children before all at one time. There are a lot more of them than there is of you. You are responsible for each one, handling individual needs for attention, support, shelter, and happiness. You will oversee the finances, handle crises, sooth the tears, and the join in the laughter. You will help everyone feel a part of a big family.

Everyone will need your undivided attention. Some are high maintenance, spoiled, unsure, stressed, shy, or outspoken. Others want to be the boss, and others want to follow.

You need the skills and personality from your parent and teacher experiences. However, many of your newly adopted children come from a broader range of backgrounds that are very different from your own. Some are older with varying degrees of trust for authority. Others are too young to know what to expect. Leading so many people with different personality quirks and needs requires serious reflection, planning, and "common horse sense" on your part. Just like a first-time parent (and often a single one at that), once reality hits, it is a very scary thought that you are now responsible for everyone.

This is definitely a new experience and responsibility. How will you handle so many people? How will you earn their trust? How will you learn to trust each of them? What does building trust look like?

When Do I Begin?

The first two months with the staff will set the tone. The process of building trust takes time and energy. The previous metaphor is meant to put you in a frame of mind that shows how suddenly everyone depends on you. You will carefully plan your course of action to begin building this important foundation for creating a family unit.

Building trust begins with your first interactions with staff members. This process takes a lot of time up front. Be yourself—friendly and positive.

The first thing that staff worry about is how much will the new boss change our culture? The first myth you will dispel—you will not change anything until you analyze and listen to the needs of the students and staff. Then, you will develop a plan together. The sooner this message gets out, the better it will be for everyone.

Respond to conversations by letting each person know how happy you are to join them. You have already examined the hard data, met with your Leadership Team, and formed ideas from your findings and discussions. Keep any judgments and opinions to yourself; bite your tongue if you have to. Your next formal interaction with the staff will require more note taking.

What Should I Do and How Should I Do It?

Who Are These People?

Mail a Letter to the Staff as Soon as Possible after Your Appointment

It will contain a friendly introduction about yourself (a full résumé is not needed here), a welcome back note, and an opening activity agenda. The sooner the letter goes to staff, the sooner the first wave of speculation is diminished about who you are and what you plan to do.

Chapter 3 discussed the need to keep the time frame for your agenda for the first days before school starts the same as last year. This appears a simple thing, but it sends a subtle message. It lets the staff know that you do not plan to change everything all at one time.

Have Teachers Complete an Expanded Typical Information Card

During the first day with teachers, when they complete the typical need-to-know things, add something new. On the information card, have the teachers place the name of their spouse or significant other living in the same home, including the names of children and pets. Here is a way to use this information: There are times when teachers are asked to go above and beyond the call of duty. For example, teachers might return to school in the evening or on the weekend to chaperone a dance or work on a committee. Perhaps a custodian volunteers to stay late to do something special—something at school that takes any one of your staff away from his or her family.

When you are new to the school, teachers will grumble when you ask them to do something that they didn't have to do with the old principal. The following letter might ease the griping. It is addressed not to the teacher, but to his or her family, including the pets, thanking them for letting the teacher do this special thing for the school. Single staff members think it's hysterical that this letter is sent to the pet. Single staff, no pets—then the letter goes directly to the staff member.

Dear Sam (husband), Mary (child), Suzy (baby),
Fluffy (cat), and Jaws (goldfish),

I want to take this opportunity to thank you for providing the support at home for Jennifer (teacher) to help us out last weekend. I realize that when she chaperoned the dance Saturday, it meant you were without her for the evening.

The dedication of teachers like Jennifer provides Somewhere High School with the highest-quality educators who consistently go above and beyond their school day. She exemplifies the commitment to her profession we all value.

It is your encouragement and understanding that helps Jennifer give so generously of her time. We are very grateful.

Sincerely,
Principal X

During your Back-to-School Time (Or Within the First Two Weeks of School), Distribute a Brief Questionnaire to Each Staff Member

> ### *Getting to Know You*
>
> Dear faculty:
>
> During the next two weeks, I will meet with you so that I can get a chance to know you a little better. Please read over the following items so that you will have time to think about questions when I ask them. If you bring the questions with you, that would help; completing them ahead of time is optional.
>
> Please arrange a 20-minute conference time, beginning (date). The school secretary will help you find a time that will work. If you cannot find a time during the day, I will be at school at 7:00 a.m. and will stay as long as needed. I plan to complete the meetings in three weeks. I look forward to our visit.
>
> Sincerely,
> Principal X

What are your favorite hobbies or activities outside school?

_____

What is your favorite part of your job?

_____

What is the distance from your home to the school?

_____

Tell me about your family.

_____

How long have you been at the school? If more than five years, what keeps you here?_____

What motivated you to teach your current grade or subject?

_____

What is the philosophy of the school?

_____

What is the greatest challenge in your classroom?

_____

What are the greatest strengths of this school?

_____

In what areas would you like to see improvement?

_____

Describe your team for me. What are the team strengths?

_____

Do you have a particular role on your team? Are you the cheerleader, the organized one, the thinker, what?_____

How many times did my predecessor visit your classroom on an informal, drop-in visit? How many times were you evaluated formally last year?

_____

What is your assessment of the standardized test scores from your students?

_____

Do you feel the standardized test scores are a true reflection of your students' actual performance? Why or why not?

_____

I want you to know that my job is to support you. What does that mean to you? In other words, what can I do that would make you feel supported?

_____

These guiding questions for teachers are not meant to be completed ahead of time but reviewed to give them time to think about how they will respond in a meeting with you. Teachers have enough forms to fill out. They don't need another one.

Ask your secretary to keep track of the schedule to ensure that everyone sets a time. (She will have to nag some of the teachers who always forget or don't want to be bothered.) The day before your meeting, ask your secretary to give another copy of the questions to the teacher to review. (Yes, only the most organized will remember to bring the original questions with them. Many will completely forget what you asked.)

Meet with Every Staff Member Individually to Begin Building Trust

In very large schools, this can be a big commitment of time. You may need to get creative about how to find 20 minutes with each teacher. Meeting with you could happen before or after school. It could be carved from time before an evening event or meeting when the teacher is on campus anyway. Because this is time taken from some other commitment of the teacher, there is another option. Hire a substitute who will rotate and cover classrooms while the teachers meet with you. It is well worth the money, time, and effort.

If you have an assistant, assign them to cover your jobs for you while you are in meetings. If you do not, schedule blocks of time when your secretary or guidance counselor can handle the little things. Your meeting should not be interrupted unless there is a severe crisis that only you can handle.

You need to know your staff and they need to know you. You must meet with everyone. Although you have met with small groups in an informal way, this is more formal with a clear agenda.

Some teachers may appear to resent the time it takes to see you, but behind your back, they will applaud the time you took to talk to each one. Once again, have snacks and beverages available. You may be taking away from a break time for them, so at least feed them.

Prepare for the meeting with staff members by doing the following:

- Review the schedule for the day.

- In large schools, you may want a picture of the teacher to attach to your notes. It is hard to keep track of teachers' names in large schools during the first month or so. If there is no picture, take one. Take advantage of advanced photography options.

- Have the teacher's file available. Review the résumé and past evaluations (see Chapter 1). This is a quick review to make your visit more productive. You'll have more information to guide other questions.

♦ Have a form with each of the planned questions or a template on your laptop so that you can take notes. (Some believe the laptop is too impersonal—you are the judge.)

Guiding Questions for the Teachers

(You will add others that get to the heart of your beliefs.) You will respond to the questions but keep your opinions to yourself for now. This is the time to get a sense of what each teacher believes and practices, both as a teacher and a team member. You may want to change some of the questions for meetings with subgroups such as custodians and teacher's aides.

Some answers from teachers may give you an extra heartbeat. Watch your body language, keep your eyes from rolling up, and smile a lot (through clenched teeth if you have to). Practice in front of the mirror on days when you meet with teachers so that you won't say, "You've got to be kidding." Instead, practice, "Oh, really?" and "I'm not sure I understand, could you explain what you just said a little more?" Keep those notes going.

Soon you will begin to see patterns emerge—find them. Organize your findings. The greatest problem with meetings such as these exists when the principal will not compile the information and draw conclusions. What system can you figure out that would help in that process? Is the information you receive from individuals the same as the conclusions you reached when you met with earlier groups? What is the same? Were there any surprises?

A caveat: Teachers are uncertain about you at this point. They may tell you what they think you want to hear. Don't worry about that. Whatever staff members say to you is just the beginning of your interaction. You need an eyeball-to-eyeball opportunity to talk to every staff member. Go with your instincts as you analyze your discussions.

Questions to Ask Yourself as You Examine Your Notes

♦ Are there teams that seem particularly together? Which ones? Why?

♦ Which teams seem to have members who "do their own thing?"

♦ Is there a common understanding of the philosophy of the school? (Don't be surprised if there is not—make a note.)

♦ Are there individuals who already have emerged as leaders?

♦ Are there individuals who don't mesh with a team? Why not?

♦ Are there any individuals with whom, at least on the surface, you felt an immediate connection and whom you could count on for help?

- Which individuals seem "with it" and describe your beliefs about students?
- What else do you want to know about each of the staff members to begin understanding the culture based on individual beliefs?
- Are staff members' classrooms visited often? How has that been organized? If not, why not?
- What do your instincts tell you about the school as a whole?
- Do you see glaring issues? Do you see areas you can work on right away?
- Which staff members are problem solvers and which ones are problem generators?
- What else could teachers tell you about themselves that you did not ask?

The Grieving Process Is Real

At the beginning stages of understanding your new staff and building relationships, you may get confusing messages. While visiting with the staff members, you may find that some of them are reserved, aloof, fairly unresponsive, or downright crabby. For the time being, there may be one explanation. The staff member is grieving for the loss of your predecessor.

The pervasiveness and depth of grieving depends on the popularity and circumstances of the previous principal's departure from the position. Factor this in as a possibility when you analyze teacher's comments.

If your predecessor was well liked and principal of the school for several years, he or she is bound to have a following. In reality, the issue is one of loss and the uncertainty of inevitable change. Each staff member will respond to the loss in a different way. For now, don't take it personally.

If you are experiencing feelings of anxiety, it may be more than just the enormousness and reality of your new job. You are also dealing with a huge change from your former position. Even if you are an experienced principal who changed schools because you requested a different school, you, too, are grieving for the loss of your previous school community. It is a natural reaction.

Factor in the potential grief as you and your new staff act and react to questions. When you meet with each of the staff members, the intent is fact finding. However, make note of your emotions and those of the people with whom you are interacting. The feelings of loss will get better over time. Understand that the emotions are real (Nolen-Larson, 1999).

Building Relationships

Celebrate

How can a principal and staff get past the emotions that exist during the transition time? Create reasons to celebrate. Celebrations can become stand-alone events or a part of a staff meeting (DuFour & Eaker, 1998).

Find out whether there is already a group in the school responsible for parties, showers, birthdays, or any other kind of recognition. If so, get the group together and begin planning. If no group has formed yet, ask for volunteers and organize them. As soon as this group meets, you may not need to oversee their ideas after the initial meeting. Perhaps there is someone who will chair the group and just keep you informed.

Celebrating is about building relationships. You can find all kinds of reasons to promote schoolwide team building. When meeting with the committee, determine the past practices. Try to raise the level of celebration up a notch from the old ways. This is one area where you can increase the expectation and create positive feelings.

This is also a time to figure out whether there are some teams who simply want to be left alone. In very large schools, particularly high schools that are huge, it is easy to lose people. Develop a way to encourage everyone's participation—even if it means that you have to personally ask individual members of the staff to join you in an after-school function. (Note: If this occurs again with the same teacher, another issue evolves. This is a teacher who needs a sit-down meeting with you to find out the real source of his or her lack of interest in participating in the group.)

Building Relationships through Classroom Visits

The most significant way to build relationships is to visit every classroom and work area consistently. Set a goal similar to that discussed in Chapter 5 to schedule yourself in classrooms. You'll note custodial work in the process.

Set a target for the number of classrooms you will visit every day.

- Informal visits should be scheduled on your calendar the same as formal ones. It is on your schedule, and nothing should interrupt it. Schedule other meetings around your classrooms visits.

- You should visit every classroom continuously, all year long. Each time, stay long enough to make notes to the teacher with a copy that you keep. If your school is large, you may have one assistant or more who shares the responsibility. It is not uncommon for principals and assistants to do well keeping to this schedule for the first semester. However, after that, it is very easy to let the hectic pace of the day get in the way. Keep the schedule you set for the first quarter of school consistently throughout the year.

◆ Visiting classrooms frequently sets a standard that tells teachers you are interested in and want to support their efforts. Leave a brief message regarding something you noticed, including something positive.

◆ Word spreads like wildfire when you visit a classroom. It's a good word.

◆ Create an organizational system that provides a way to leave a note for the teacher with a copy for you. (Imagine the telephone message pads that have a carbonless way to keep copies of messages.) In this way, you can keep track of what you said to whom and when you said it.

◆ Spend the money to create carbonless notepads for informal observations (see Chapter 5) using a half sheet. Create a template for as much information as possible. Hand write what you need to say.

◆ Do not return to your office to complete the information. Once you get to your office, who knows how long it will be before you can get back to this note? It's a logistical nightmare. Write what you need to say at the moment. Leave it on the teacher's desk. Take your carbon copy back to the office and develop a system so that your secretary can file it in the teacher's file. (These notes are invaluable when you write the teacher's evaluations and assessments.)

Drop-In Visit Note

XYZ Middle School

Principal:_____

Date:_____ Time: _____ Teacher's name: _____
Class: _____

I visited your classroom today and noticed: (something positive)

Please schedule a time with my secretary to see me—I have a couple of questions.

Would you bring your lesson plan book with you?

Would you bring your assessment book with you?

Other: _____

(Circle the questions that you may want to include).

♦ Create an organizational system that keeps track of the classrooms you have visited. Especially in large schools, it is easy to forget some people. Teachers who have classrooms away from the main building are often the forgotten ones. (They will be the first to tell you they are neglected.)

List every teacher's name. Then, as you go into the classroom and note the date at a quick glance you will be able to see the teachers you are forgetting.

Classroom Visitation Log

Teacher name: _____ Room #: _____ Date: _____

Note left (see file)

_____

_____

_____

_____

♦ Your secretary can help you with follow-up meetings. The first visit is not the time to get heavy handed in your visits with teachers, when you are unsure of what is going on in the classroom.

♦ If the first visit caused you some concern, the follow-up visit should occur within the next two weeks.

♦ Listen patiently as the staff members explain what they are doing, and answer any questions you may have. Take notes to use at a later time.

♦ Spend time with students. Every student should know who you are.

♦ Encourage students to talk about what they are learning.

Questions and Answers

Q: What should I say in my introductory letter to the staff?

A: Be brief, be yourself, and include a brief outline of the opening agenda. For more assistance, ask your mentor to fax you the one that he or she used and modify it to fit your needs.

Q: What conclusions can I draw from my meeting with staff members?

A: Family issues are often the explanation for a staff member who is unusually stressed by their responsibilities outside school. This can sometimes explain the behavior of teachers who, on the surface, give the appearance of a lack of interest in or dedication to the job. In reality, they have a very full plate. It is good to know that before assigning a person with a lot of responsibilities to a leadership role, unless they volunteer.

When teachers are unable to articulate the philosophy of the school, you will spend time analyzing what seems to be the problem. Are the teachers so new that they haven't a sense of the philosophy? Do teachers say they have no idea? Why not? Find out and plan to fix it.

Q: Meeting with individuals is another huge time commitment. How can I fit it all in? Is it worth it?

A: It is a huge amount of time, and it is worth it. Think of the alternative. Your staff will see you when you have your first staff meeting, and they may get a glimpse of you passing in the hallway (if you have a large school). How long would it take you to sit down with each one to get to know him or her? Just like the people on the tour bus in Chapter 1, you will never know some staff members otherwise. At the very least, it may take months before you know them. This is most time-consuming when you are the new one.

You can fit it in if you get creative with the time—for example, by hiring a substitute teacher to go from staff member to staff member in 20-minute intervals on a prearranged schedule. Your secretary can help you with the scheduling process.

Q: My school is too large to get everyone to celebrate at one time. What should I do?

A: Everyone is required to attend your staff meetings. Celebrate then. Cut your meeting down (teachers can read), celebrate something, feed people snacks and beverages, and let those who want to stay and mingle do so. Then, on your staff meeting day, meet, celebrate, and let everyone go home an unannounced 10–15 minutes early. Every once in a while, use this strategy.

Q: I know I have to get into classrooms, but all my colleagues say it is too hard. They can't get out of their offices. How can I handle the time commitment?

A: This chapter addressed building trust. Review Chapter 5 to see whether the time issue is an organizational one. Otherwise, classroom visits must be scheduled as if they were important meetings—they are. You are setting a precedent for the time you put into this necessary responsibility.

Parents, teachers, and students will quickly learn that you are not available during the hours of ___ to ___ every day. How else will you establish yourself as a continuing and interested presence if you aren't demonstrating the importance of watching instructional practices? Besides, you are learning unfamiliar curriculum, instruction, and assessment at the same time.

Your secretary can tell those who need you that you are in the classroom. Everyone will respect that choice. Stand firm on your classroom visitation time from the beginning, and pretty soon people will learn. It is much harder if you try to implement this strategy later on. Begin on day one.

Not only do teachers need to see you, so do the students. In larger schools, students often never see the principal. Most of them barely know the principal's name. This is a case of establishing your priorities; you need to be with teachers and students during on-the-clock time.

You easily can be held hostage in your office. All of your adopted children need you all of the time, whenever they are on a break. This could mean every period from the time school starts until school ends. Teachers who want to see you when you are in classrooms will figure out a way to see you before or after school. Your secretary can schedule parent meetings around your classroom visitation time. Supervisors will not argue with your lack of availability if you are in classrooms. They will let you know if they can't wait.

 **Survival Tips**

In the early stages of getting to know you, teachers have a fairly concise way of judging whether to trust you. Interviews with numerous teachers revealed the following statements as they answered the question "What does an administrator have to do in order to build trust among the staff?" During your first few months, the answers will be fairly concrete and very teacher-centered.

- "When I send a student to you for discipline, then it is because I have already tried everything I know. If somehow you don't think my decision was the right one, let me know why. Don't just send the student back to me without an explanation. I am asking for support."

- "Support me with a parent when I need someone to back me up. If the parent starts pointing the blame at me, and you don't defend me, then it makes me look bad."

- "Never reveal my conversations with you unless it is something positive, or we agreed that others need to become involved."

- "Do what you said you were going to do, when you said you would do it. Don't forget" (Daft & Lengel, 2000).

- "If you have an issue with me about something, do not have that conversation in front of anyone else. If we need to talk about something, do it out of 'ear's reach' of anyone else."

- "In a staff meeting, do not scold the group for the issues with just one or a small few. It is demeaning."

- "If someone "messed up," then talk only to them. I can't trust someone who gets mad at everyone for the mistakes of one or two people and makes a 'big deal' out of it in front of everyone. If we all didn't do something we were supposed to, then at least treat us like adults."

- "Don't pretend to be an expert on something you know nothing about. When you ask for my help and my opinion, I begin building trust. This tells me that you trust my judgment and my ideas, so it works both ways."

- "I need to know that you value me; let me know in a variety of ways."

Based on what teachers said about trust building, you can do several things to build areas of trust.

- In their book Fusion Leadership, Richard Daft and Robert Lengel state, "Be absolutely honest, both with yourself and with others" (2000, p. 184). Understand what trust means to your staff. Respond honestly to their expectations of trust.

- Establish a system so that the receiving administrator of the students knows what the teacher expects the administrator to do. For example, you may have a place on the referral form that says, "What do you expect the administrator to do?" If the teacher wants you to suspend a student from school and you think that is too harsh, then get back to the teacher as soon as the teacher can discuss the issue with you. Teachers perceive a disconnect between what they expect should happen and what does happen as a breakdown in trust.

- Make it standard procedure that you never sit in on a parent–teacher conference without first meeting with the teacher or team and reviewing the information to determine exactly what each person plans to say. Decide what your role will be. This can be accomplished by giving yourself and the team 10–15 minutes before the meeting with the parent to decide what everyone wants to accomplish. The key question to ask the group is, "What do we want the outcome of this conference to accomplish?" Then you are prepared. In high-stakes times, conferences can be very challenging, and you all need a plan. Teachers feel supported, and you receive a notch on your "trust-building belt."

- Find out the details, the individuals involved, and your expectations for solving a problem that may result in frustration. For example, you set a deadline for a completed form. Several teachers didn't turn them in. Find a way to communicate individually with each one. If the problem persists, talk to them one on one. With enough nagging, you hope the problem won't continue. The point is to stick with the individuals, not the group, for "nagging."

- Admit when you don't know something and ask teachers for their suggestions on issues when solving problems.

- Make the hard decisions when you have to. Some things are just not negotiable.

The process of grieving is very real. Accept it as part of the behavior exhibited. However, if there is a negative attitude toward you by anyone on the staff that lasts more than a month, it is time for a heart-to-heart talk about the real source of the problem.

Surviving large groups in your new family requires you to recognize your idiosyncrasies and the crazy behavior of your adoptees and to laugh. Huge amounts of time can be wasted trying to fix every quirk. Analyze the difference between things you can laugh off and those you can't.

When forming and implementing celebrations, try to make them better than teachers' previous experiences.

- Perhaps you can scrounge up additional sources of funding or business partners who will donate door prizes to make the celebration look different (Deal & Peterson, 1999).

- Keep the actual celebration short, with time for staff to spend time together afterward. Stick around. Teachers need an opportunity to interact informally with you as well.

- If you serve on the celebrations committee, that reinforces its importance. As soon as the committee seems ready to work on its own, you can meet periodically with the chair of this group.

- Involve the whole staff in their areas of responsibility. A grade level or team may be responsible for refreshments during committee-assigned times.

- Invite dignitaries to any event at which staff members receive special recognition: receiving a grant, achieving National Board Certification, winning a content-specific award. When the award is presented by someone in a "high position," it adds additional importance.

- If the staff do not want to be bothered with the celebration of things, then don't call it a celebration. Call it a staff meeting, during which time you celebrate. Most union contracts require teachers to attend staff meetings called by the principal. How surprising that a staff meeting actually can be fun!

- If this is an area that is already strong and functions well, leave it alone. It's one less thing for you to worry about. Could you add a little something of your own to the celebration or ceremony?

Visit a specific number of classrooms every day and keep to your schedule.

- As soon as teachers see you in their classrooms—especially when you leave them a positive note—it sends a strong message that you are interested in what they are doing.

- As soon as you start letting meetings or minor issues interfere with your visits, the message is also clear: You don't do what you say will do. It also sends the signal that you don't care as much about what goes on in their classrooms as you said you did.

- If you go into classrooms only for formal assessments, you are severely handicapped at the formal evaluation time. You only see the "dog-and-pony evaluation time show" and have no way of knowing what goes on during every other day of instruction. Remember how you felt when an administrator rarely watched you teach.

- The school will only become more successful if you have competent staff. How will you know whether the teacher is consistently competent if you watch a teacher teach only the number of times specified in the union contract?

Summary

Successful administrators recognize and practice relationship building within the school environment to create trust among teachers and between the administrator and staff. Building relationships and trust is a long process and may not happen for a long time. It does not happen quickly.

The administrator must demonstrate fundamental characteristics of trustworthiness such as being honorable, truthful, fair, and reasonable. Trust building does not require a lot of "cutesy" overt activities, although for some groups, it works fine. Trust building occurs through continuous positive interactions among individual staff members, the principal, and the assistant principal.

A principal or assistant principal is someone who consistently does the right thing with the best interests of the staff, students, and parents at heart. In reality, only the principal is privy to some sensitive information when making decisions, so the staff may not understand that you are implementing the right thing and that challenge is a given. However, openly discussing the issues and rationale behind decision making helps staff to recognize why unpopular decisions occur (Daft & Lengel, 2000). Then, when a principal must say, "trust me on this one," staff members, for the most part, will live with the decision.

Patience and understanding are important components of the administrator's job. Behaviors that appear unsupportive of you, the new guy or gal, may simply be the result of a staff member grieving for your predecessor, whom they had learned to trust, and the looming change that they believe will occur. Over time, you will win most of them over. (Those you don't will probably move to another school.)

Building trust occurs when teachers know you are in a position to support them with their students, parents, and each other. A systematic, predictable, and unrelenting schedule that ensures you are in classrooms often and consistently sends an important message. You will watch instructional practices, you will provide the support teachers need, and you will know what you are talking about. At the same time, you demonstrate your credibility.

Questions for Reflection

1. Describe what building trust means to you. List the characteristics and examples of how someone earned your trust. How could you use these same characteristics in your interactions with staff members? What characteristics develop when there is a lack of trust in an organization as a whole or with team members as a small group? How would you turn a lack of trust into trust building?

2. Discuss how you would organize the information provided by teachers during your informal meetings with them so that you could draw conclusions about the school. What alternative would you devise as a way to get to know each of your staff members during the first two months of school?

3. Discuss how you would respond to teachers who are not receptive to the idea of joining others to celebrate. What other ideas can you think of to get staff members together to build trust in yourself and others?

4. Discuss how you would avoid the "office hostage" problem of the principal. Describe ways that you could get to know the students.

5. Describe how you would stick to your commitment to visit a specific number of classrooms every day, including the teachers who might be located away from the main building.

7

Studying and Learning Through Observations: Where Is Everyone— Same Book, Same Chapter, Same Page, or on Another Planet?

(First Two Months after the Teachers Arrive)

The observation process is one of the most important functions of your job. Through methodical visits, you can analyze every teacher's commitment to the improvement of each student. This lets you know whether the teacher follows the vision of the school, understands the book, and is on the same chapter, same page, or some other planet.

Consistently evaluating what happens in classrooms determines the success of student progress, builds trust between you and the faculty, establishes your credibility, provides the basis on which to create staff development, and determines the direction of the School Improvement Plan. The foundation for curriculum, instruction, and assessment begins in the classroom, and it is up to you, the school principal, to ensure that the highest-quality teachers guide the students.

Jo and Joseph Blase are among the many authors who have reported on the importance of teacher observations and conferences. Their studies describe the "benefits of developing reflective, collaborative, problem-solving contexts for dialogue about instruction" (1998, p. 4). Observing teachers and providing helpful feedback is a critical part of your job as principal.

The range of abilities, potential, and talent is as diverse as the number of people on your staff. The range of your abilities to evaluate teachers is as diverse as your personal background of experiences and your understanding of what effective teaching practices look like.

When Do I Begin?

Focused observations occur during the first two months of school. You have already visited each classroom more than one time. In September, you visited the classrooms to become familiar with the culture. You began to establish trust at that point and looked for positive ways to recognize teachers' hard work. During each visit, you left a note that recognized that you paid attention to what happened in the classroom as you watched the teachers work with the curriculum, instruction, and assessment (see Chapter 6). At this point, you recognize commonalities and differences among teachers' styles, presentations, and expectations.

What Should I Do and How Should I Do It?

By the second month of school, your visits to classrooms will become more focused. In November and December, you must be ready to accurately assess teachers who are not tenured with a formal evaluation (see Chapter 8).

Observing Teachers
Who Are Outside Your Own Teaching Field

The challenging part of the observation process comes when you evaluate a teacher through an overview of the classroom; however, you may not have a clear understanding of each subject area. For example, if you were a language arts teacher, how do you effectively evaluate a physics teacher? If you were a social science teacher, how do you effectively evaluate the music teacher? How do you effectively evaluate the teachers of special needs students unless you understand and learn the complex arena of exceptional education?

Before you can adequately evaluate teachers and provide meaningful feedback, you need to build your own background in areas outside your fields of expertise. Who better to learn from than the master teachers who already work in your school? Because you are new to the school, how do you find the master teachers?

Ask three questions of yourself and others. First, ask members of the Leadership Team to define a master teacher according to the culture of the school. Second, how do *you* define a master teacher? Is there a disconnect between the level of expectation that exists in the school of your appointment and your belief?

If you currently work in a school, ask yourself the same questions. If you were to watch highly effective teachers in your existing workplace, whom would you select and why? Put the formal assessment requirement of the district aside for the moment as you sort out your own beliefs.

Once you identify the master teachers, let them know that you need to watch them work—to learn from them. In some school districts, tenured teachers often, by contract, do not require formal evaluations. However, in the early phases of your appointment, this is the time to learn and to build your background. You demonstrate a level of trust when you ask a master teacher if you can watch him or her in order to learn.

Study and observe master teachers at work until you get a sense of what effective teaching looks like. Master teachers can answer questions you may generate as you learn strategies for instruction in the content areas. In this way, by the time you watch the newer teachers, you will be able to provide them with helpful feedback, not just generic comments.

Because you are new to the school and just getting to know the staff, what characteristics and behaviors can help to sort out the various groups with whom you work?

Master Teachers, Mental Dinosaurs, and Generation Y (twentysomethings)

When watching and interacting with teachers, you will discover that within the range of experience of staff members, there are three fairly distinct groups of teachers. They are described here as *master teachers, mental dinosaurs,* and *Generation Y.* Recognize that they exist and that each group requires a different way to assess and subsequently provide support. In their book *Boomers, X'er's, and Other Strangers,* Rick and Kathy Hicks (1999) identified characteristics of the different age groups that are part of a school. The importance of understanding each group becomes helpful with issues of communication and acceptance of individual differences among the staff. It also helps you to recognize why some people drive you crazy.

You will establish different goals for yourself in preparation for discussions during the upcoming observations. The preconference, observation, and postconference discussions will set in motion your expectations for effective teaching. They also will provide the vehicle that drives your support for teachers.

In Chapter 6, you interviewed the teachers. Now that you have seen them at work, you can use what you know, combined with your observations, to draw initial conclusions.

Master teachers are your most experienced and effective teachers. Who are they and how should you recognize them?

- When analyzing individual testing data, these teachers demonstrate impressive gains for their students. If every student does not meet the teacher's expectations, they give a logical explanation.

- During your individual meetings with teachers during September or October (detailed in Chapter 2), master teachers describe strategies used and future plans for improving their instructional practices.

- Master teachers' names are used frequently in conversations with other members of the staff for their teaching practices and positive interaction with other staff members, students, and parents.

- Master teachers are recognized by students, who make a point of wanting to be in that teacher's class.

- Master teachers consistently contribute to the overall effectiveness of their teams and the school.

- Master teachers clearly articulate their instructional approaches and expected outcomes for their lessons.

- Master teachers describe how they incorporate testing strategies into their regular instructional practices. They do not let standardized testing drive their teaching focus.
- Master teachers reflect on their craft and consistently develop a plan to improve instruction. They can explain their plan.
- Master teachers are generally willing and able to help you. They are good about thinking issues through and brainstorming options for implementing ideas.
- Master teachers volunteer to mentor and coach other teachers.
- Master teachers "know their stuff." You can trust their judgment.
- Master teachers are "on the same page." They are writing the book.

True Story

> I was appointed during the summer. In July, I had a teacher come to me and ask for a meeting. When we started talking, I realized I had someone who was a master teacher and someone I could count on for help. It was obvious he wanted to help me with my vision. I am very lucky he came forward. I continue to rely on him to keep me up to speed on his area of expertise. Not only are we on the same page, we are rewriting the book.
>
> —High school principal

Mental dinosaurs have been in the business forever. They know they have "been there, done that" and generally don't want to go back through the cycle one more time. This type of dinosaur is not age related. It is a mental mind-set and attitude.

- Mental dinosaurs see no benefit to themselves or their students from redoing and changing their past practices.
- Mental dinosaurs usually want to be left alone.
- Mental dinosaurs will listen to what you tell them to do, nod appropriately, and return to their classrooms and continue to do what they have always done.
- Mental dinosaurs cope by using passive resistance behaviors.
- Mental dinosaurs often see themselves as dinosaurs. Their personal behavior demonstrates resignation to their role. They usually believe that because the instruction they have used in the past works (according to their personal standards), there is no need to invest in the effort to change.

- Mental dinosaurs often say to themselves or to others, "I was doing what I do before this 'new whippersnapper' got here, and I'll do it after he is gone." They probably have ties and underwear that are older than you.

- Mental dinosaurs need a lot of encouragement. They often do not see themselves as valued by the administration or the organization as a whole. At one time in their careers, they may have been seen as a master teacher but feel they are no longer in that place.

- Mental dinosaurs need to know you value them. It is worth a try to get them to come around to a new idea or belief, but it won't happen unless they receive personal attention and opportunities to contribute to the school in positive ways.

- Mental dinosaurs usually want to help you but don't think you want their help.

- Mental dinosaurs often demonstrate their need to be needed by mothering those "new young things."

- Mental dinosaurs have "heard of the book."

True Story

A veteran teacher volunteered to be my mentor during my first year. She willingly shared all of her black-line masters of worksheets with me (even though I was not quite sure what to do with all of them). She was so nice. She invited me to her house for dinner. She even gave me the calendar she used so I could plan my activities for the year. In this way, I knew that the second week in March "we" make homemade butter.

—Elementary school teacher

Generation Y teachers are usually young, new, clueless, and scared. Frequently, new teachers place themselves in extremely stressful situations all at one time: (1) graduating from college; (2) planning a wedding; (3) getting married; (4) moving; (5) finding a job; (6) finding a place to live; (7) learning to live with someone; and, surprise of all surprises, (7) paying their own bills.

They arrive in their new jobs already stressed because the real world hits them and they are faced with the expectation that they are a grown-up. Yet, in spite of all that, they have tremendous potential if given the right resources and support.

Remember the story in Chapter 6 about adopting a school full of children? Here they are. You need a whole lot of patience, Mom or Dad.

- New teachers usually come to school with very limited personal supplies or materials. They assume the school will provide them with the same stockpile of resources that veteran teachers possess. They grew up with parents who provided them with everything they wanted—the same expectations transfer to the workplace.

- *Improvise* is a new word for Generation Yers.

- When new teachers enter their classrooms for the first time and their expectations fall short of reality, several behavioral possibilities emerge:
  - They run as fast as possible to the school secretary and give them a list of everything they need or want—over and over.
  - If they don't get what they want, they whine to their colleagues.
  - Often their attitude is "I want what I want, when I want it—and I want it *now*!"

- When faced with multiple responsibilities at one time, Generation Yers may exhibit many of the same behaviors as the overwhelmed administrator (identified in Appendix A).

- Generation Yers forget everything they learned during their internships because this school doesn't do things exactly the same way.

- Generation Yers quickly develop information overload. In addition to the mountains of papers they received during preservice days, their team members often willingly pile one page on top of the other "in case they need it." In the rush of getting school started, the helping teachers don't have time to provide information on how to use these treasured activities.

- Generation Yers keep waiting for someone to tell them what to do and how to do it. Everyone assumes they should know. They panic.

- To make bad matters worse, you continue to drop in to watch them teach, and now you will formally observe them. War stories abound. They believe every one of them.

- Frequently, new teachers are unaware of the protocol in their new culture.

- Generation Yers dress the same way they dressed in college: casual at best.

- Generation Yers won't ask or adhere to cultural standards because they never learned the importance of adapting to existing cultures.

- Generation Yers often see no connection between their personal needs and the school's accepted practices.

- Personal needs outweigh the school's and the students' needs.
- Generation Yers read the book, passed a test on the book, and it's in a box somewhere.
- Now it is you who has underwear older than them.

True Story

A new teacher came to me the second day on the job. "I looked around at the other teachers on my team and I don't have nearly everything they have in their rooms. It's not fair. I'm a new teacher and I don't have anything." Of course, we had given her adequate materials and supplies, but they were the basics. She wanted 10 years of acquired materials and supplies that her teammates had collected.

—Elementary school principal

Focused Drop-In Visits Allow You to Begin Learning about Curriculum, Instruction, and Assessment

You make efficient use of your time when you expect all teachers to put their assessment records and lesson plans in a place where you can access them without disturbing their class, even during drop-in visits. After the first round, you will begin looking for key indicators of effective instruction and begin asking direct questions for clarification of instructional practices you may not understand.

This information provides you with the background you need to conduct knowledgeable and thoughtful formal observations and postobservation conferences. The following strategies will help you begin to learn and understand unfamiliar content areas.

- In each grade level or department, begin with the master teachers. Proceed through the department or grade level from the most senior to the least senior teacher. In this way, you can establish a standard that demonstrates current accepted practices within that department or grade level.
- When you are on a learning curve, watch teachers in a block of selected classes so that you can sequence your learning experiences. For example, visit all classrooms in a grade level, such as all kindergarten classes, all seventh-grade or all high school math classrooms, beginning with the resident kindergarten, seventh-grade,

or math expert and proceeding to the least experienced teacher (horizontal teams). Then, observe all classes in a single content area. For example, visit all classes in 9th- through 12th-grade algebra or advanced English, watching the progression of instruction from one year to the next (vertical teams).

- When assessing teaching practices in a methodical sequence, you have a better way to make comparisons among those within a department or grade level. Your conclusions will more clearly identify the range of teachers who meet quality standards.

- During your first months on the job, you need a strong understanding of each grade or department compared to each other. It is much more difficult to wrap your arms around current effective practices if you randomly drop into any classroom that you find at the moment.

- Define the areas you want to study in each classroom. A quick glance around and a couple of minutes of watching won't give you enough information to help you out during conference time. Observation by window peeking doesn't work either. Stay long enough to make your time worthwhile.

- Create your own form that you can use for note taking. Chapter 6 provided a quick note to leave the teacher; however, you need more concrete information, even during a drop-in visit.

- A specific focus for each round of visits will help you determine areas of strength and areas to improve. The following informal visit form helps you to focus and may provide ideas you can use.

Focused Observation for Drop-In Visits

Teacher name:_____ Date: **Don't forget** Time: _____

What is visible for student and teacher resources in the environment?
_____ Plenty _____ Adequate _____ Not much—find out why

What do you see to support your impression?
_____

What is the organizational structure of the classroom?
_____

Teacher:
_____Organized _____ Searching for what is needed Ask why?

Students:

_____ Meaningfully engaged _____ Unstructured _____ Unorganized

What is the interaction between the teacher and students?
_____ Interactive, positive _____ Passive, none
_____Teacher is harsh, negative

Transition time from the time the bell rings for the start of class until the teacher begins instruction: _____ minutes.

Lesson plans were
_____ Clear _____ Vague
_____ Unexplainable _____ The lesson matched the plan

Student assessments were
_____ Clear _____ Incomplete

Did the lesson plans and student assessments match by date and content?
_____

Please make an appointment to see me in the next two days so that we can discuss my visit.

Additional notes to use during conferences:

_____
_____
_____
_____

- Take time to complete your drop-in observation form before you return to your office. Give the form to your secretary, who will file it in the teacher's file.

- Each time you make a drop-in visit, note whether anything changed from the previous visit. Has anything in the environment changed? Is the teacher–student interaction the same?

- Drop-in visits should occur during different class times.

- Time as many visits as possible around transition times: those times when students come into or leave the class. You are looking for the amount of time it takes teachers to begin instructing or how soon students start packing up to leave.

- The more notes you compile, the more effective conferences become. The more effective the conference, the greater your credibility and the more meaningful support you can offer the teacher.

Drop-In Visits for Master and Veteran Teachers

- In some cultures, master and veteran teachers are on the bottom of the list for drop-in visits. They need to understand that you will stop by from time to time. There is no point in surprising them.

- Master teachers are rarely concerned about you watching them teach. Some of the teachers already may have participated in your Leadership Team. They are aware of your intention to thoroughly understand each area of the school.

- Ineffective teachers often are worried that you are trying to catch them doing something wrong.

- Each grade level, department, and course requires very different expectations of student performance and teaching strategies. Make notes about your findings.

- You want to determine the instructional strategies, assessment techniques, and student interactions that occur between effective teachers and students in areas outside your area of expertise. By watching master teachers first, they can begin training you.

First Formal Observations Begin:
November and December

Begin as soon as possible during the year, but no later than the beginning of November, or you will run out of time before the holiday break. (Follow the contractual timelines to the letter.)

There are two strategies for scheduling observations. You and your secretary can develop the schedule, or the teachers can sign up for an observation time. As a former assistant principal, you already participated in the process of formal observations.

Because you and your assistant (if you have one) are developing your new partnership, you will take time to discuss in detail your expectations and outcomes for each person being assessed. Both you and your assistant will agree on which teachers you want each to observe. In addition, you will both agree on strategies for observation that extend beyond the official form of the district.

The Role of the Assistant (If You Have One or More)
in Formal Observations

The division of labor for observations varies depending on your needs. One method is to have the assistant observe teachers who are in the assistant's area of expertise and teachers who have not emerged as struggling. Large schools, especially high schools, assign assistants to observe an area of their expertise, a department, or a grade level. Because the ultimate responsibility for reappointment rests with you, ideally, as principal, you will observe all first-year teachers, those who are up for tenure at the end of the year, and struggling teachers.

If that isn't possible, then all of the teachers who fall into the groups just noted require special preconferencing between you and your assistant to formulate an observation plan. You and your assistant will compare your combined notes from your drop-in visits. As you make the observation assignments, you will identify any areas of strengths, areas to improve, and teachers' practices that you don't understand.

You will meet at the conclusion of the observations and agree on the written statements included "on the record." Until you are completely comfortable with your assistant's assessment of teachers, you will always know the conclusions reached with each staff member (including noninstructional staff). In this way, there are no surprises when the end-of-year final assessments are written.

Preconference for Nontenured Staff
(15–20 minutes)

What should you prepare for the conference?

- For all teachers who are in their second year, review their previous observations. (If you are lucky, your predecessor was a thorough observer, note taker, and document collector. If not, it begins with you.)
- Review your predecessor's notes regarding the status of the teacher. Is this a teacher who is eligible for tenured status at the end of the year? Is this a teacher who is new to the field?
- Review the dates, times, and notes from your informal observations over the last two months, including those of your assistant (if you have one).
- Review the informal observation forms that you intend to use to supplement your observation. (You may choose to use blank paper to jot down notes, forms that focus on specific areas for observation, or both.)
- Review the formal teacher assessment instrument from the district.
- Review any standardized testing data that provides information about the teacher and you to discuss.

What should the teacher bring to the preconference?

- Lesson plans for the specific lesson being observed
- A copy of the lesson plans from the beginning of the year
- Student assessment book
- Seating chart for you that provides the seating for the day of observation
- Copy of the daily and weekly schedule
- Names of students with special needs or those considered "inclusion" students. Where they are located on the seating chart?

What should you expect to have learned at the end of the preconference?

- How lesson plans are written for each day
- How the lesson plan describes the observation lesson
- All assessment methods
- The assessment plan for the observation lesson
- The adaptations planned for students who "don't get it" during the lesson.

- The names and seating of students with whom the teacher needs your observational information. (This request is common for attention deficit, unmotivated, behaviorally disordered, and unusually low-performing students.)

What should the teacher expect at the end of the preconference?

- A review of the districts document used during the evaluation process.

- A clear understanding of your expectations—for example, will you look for specific areas that are not on the district form? What are they?

- A clear understanding that observations are a way to provide support.

- An explanation of how and why you will take additional notes.

Setting the Scene for Observation

Request that the teacher place the following information at your observation station:

- The completed lesson plans for the year that you looked at during the preconference. (If they are on the computer, then require a full set of hard-copy pages in a file or binder.)

- All student assessments, both formal (standardized testing information for the class) and informal (end-of-unit tests and other authentic assessments).

- Clarify with the teacher where you are expected to sit in the classroom and when.

Observation Time (45–60 Minutes)

- Establish a time for observation that includes student transition time from one class to the other at the beginning or ending of the class period. This extended time becomes valuable. New or struggling teachers often flounder during transitions.

- You may already know or have heard of struggling teachers. For those teachers, make sure you are in the classroom from the beginning until the end of the entire lesson (at least). Anyone can maintain a "dog-and-pony" show for about 45 minutes—longer than that, you can see the real classroom. (That's the value of drop-in visits.)

- If you are in a school that is not departmentalized, determine the content area you want to observe. For example, at the elementary school level, you may ask to observe guided reading during every teacher's observation because you are not sure how reading groups are established and students assessed in those groups. Perhaps the department or grade level had adopted a new math program and you want to see and learn how the program works; schedule for that time with every teacher.

Additional Observation Strategies

- ◆ A second hand on your watch will aid you in determining exactly how much time teachers and students spend engaging in different activities. Exact times aid in the postconference details in such areas as transitions when students enter the class until instruction begins and the length of teacher talk compared to the length of student talk within a lesson. Also, collecting data on special needs children requires frequency and duration information. (How many times to they do this "annoying thing" and for how long?)

- ◆ A tally sheet helps with additional data, such as the number of times a teacher repeats a phrase or quirk (teacher says, "Umm" or "OK" when responding to a student answer, for example, 25 times in 15 minutes).

- ◆ A sheet that identifies the seating arrangement and whether a boy or girl occupies that seat aids in the postconference in areas such as which students were asked questions or scolded for something. (Develop a code to help you interpret the information during the postconference time.)

- ◆ Determine how the teacher provides for inclusion students, such as modifying the assignments, providing preferential seating, or giving additional wait time to respond to questions.

- ◆ While observing, stay long enough to multitask. As soon as you are seated, create an area where you can look at the lesson plans. (The teacher gave you an explanation about how the plans are written, but when you see instruction, do the lesson plans make sense?)

- ◆ Look at plans and assessments at the same time, stay long enough in the classroom to accomplish these tasks before you leave the room. Place your findings in your notes to use during the postconference.

- ◆ Identify two or three children from the list of students in the class. Examine their classroom records, portfolios, grade books, or anything available that provides you with a direct connection from the teacher's instruction through to the assessment piece. Is there a clear path that makes sense? You don't need to follow every child—there is not the time. A cross-section of student work gives you a thumbnail sketch of the teacher's management system. If a red flag goes up, then you and the teacher can arrange another conference to review other records of students.

Postconference for Nontenured Staff

By the time you become a principal, you know the formal drill for postconferences. Formal evaluations get to some key indicators of a successful lesson; however, there is much more that should be discussed.

Is there anything from your drop-in visits that is consistent with your formal observations? It is not uncommon for a beginning teacher to experience challenges in one or both of the following areas: classroom management and organization.

If your timing revealed that it took the teacher five minutes to begin instruction from the time all the students were seated, calculate the total number of minutes wasted for the year. The more specific the information, the more teachers will understand your point.

Example

> Principal to teacher: I noticed that the students waited for you to start the lesson for five minutes. How else can you use that time?
>
> Teacher to principal: I have to take roll, collect and record homework assignments.
>
> Principal to teacher: Actually, if we calculate five minutes every day for the 185 days we have in a year, we get how many minutes wasted during the year? (That is near 925 minutes, or about 15.5 hours, or over two days of class). So, how could the students use the time more effectively and use your time more efficiently? How can you figure out a solution? Your mentor can give you suggestions. (You may have ideas).

The teacher's questioning also may reveal that he or she calls on more boys than girls, calls on more students on the right-hand side of the room (teacher stands at the right side of the overhead and doesn't turn to the students on the left), or stands still so that students out of the teacher's peripheral vision are left out.

You can use tally marks and notations on the seating chart to indicate that negative statements are made more frequently to specific students more than others. Ask the teacher to explain.

What should teachers expect at the end of the postconference?

- They should realize that you are committed to supporting them and helping them grow professionally.

- They should understand that you are there to support them by providing positive feedback and additional resources when needed.

- They should hear about very specific issues that identify ways to improve. If you do not have specific suggestions (you may not know what to recommend), connect them with someone you trust to give good advice, such as the teacher's mentor or school specialist.

- They should have the knowledge that you took whatever time was necessary to provide specific feedback. You admitted if you didn't have the solution to a problem but found someone who would help.

- They should receive a written plan for improvement. The plan can become very formal, such as the one that the district provides when teachers require specific, detailed, and documented plans. Or the plan may be more informal—for example, you write, "Develop a way that provides meaningful activities for the first five minutes of the class. Five days from now please e-mail me the activities you implemented based on this meeting."

What should you expect at the end of the postconference?

- You clearly communicated the results of your observation.

- You kept clear and precise notes concerning any specific suggestions, including people you will contact, timelines to follow, and a follow-up drop-in visit within the next two weeks.

- You will communicate, in writing, to the contact person and the teacher, within the next three days, whom you assigned to help, what you expect them to do, and your plans for follow-up. (E-mail works best, if you can—keep a copy for the teacher's records. Develop a system to keep track of the dates you assigned on your calendar.)

- Follow up on what you said you would do. Don't forget.

Recognizing and Working with Inexperienced and Ineffective Teachers

The most time-consuming and potentially frustrating experience occurs when you recognize that you have an ineffective teacher. You face a difficult decision. What are your conclusions at this time? What can be fixed? What is harder to fix? What seems beyond fixing?

This teacher usually has three or fewer years of experience. Before you know it, the time will hit that requires making a decision about whether to re-appoint this teacher. What do you conclude after the first three months? What is your plan of action? At this time, you draw some conclusions.

If the teacher seems salvageable,

- Concentrate on one area at a time to fix.
- Create an informal improvement plan.
- Move quickly; bring the mentor and teacher together to discuss the improvement plan.
- Methodically visit the classroom frequently. Schedule frequent follow-up meetings with the teacher.

If it is too soon to tell, but you don't have a good feeling about this teacher,

- Study the lesson plans and the assessments.
- Get into the classroom more frequently.
- Bring the mentor and teacher together to discuss a plan.
- Develop a formal improvement plan. As part of the plan, require weekly lesson plans and assessment files that are turned in and read by you or an assistant.
- When it comes time to make a decision about the teacher for next year, use your formal and informal assessments and discussions with your key support people, such as your assistant. Trust your instincts.
- If you don't think the teacher will work out in the school and you maintain the teacher for another year, there is a huge chance you will say the same thing a year from now. This is in spite of the formal plan, large amounts of support, and all.

If the teacher seems to have potential for instruction but does not get along with others,

- Find out more about the interactions with others—what is the problem?
- You will need a heart-to-heart talk with the teacher, gentle but firm. Make it clear that the issue is serious.

- Measuring this is a challenge. Figure out ways to observe the teacher's interaction with others such as joining the team for lunch and team meetings.
- Gather more information and meet again before the winter holiday. Give the teacher time to process the problem.
- Meet soon after the winter break to discuss the teacher's plan for improving his or her relationships with others. Don't let this issue slip away. Eventually, you may need to recommend that this teacher might find another team in another school a better fit.

True Story

I can't believe the times that another teacher will come to me and complain about a colleague. I listen to the story and when I discuss the same story with the colleague, the stories aren't even close to being consistent. The colleague wants to know, "Who said that?" Or "I never did that." When one team member after another tells me stories of the same person with the same issues, something has to change. If I am going to build a school, I have to have people who can work together.

—Elementary school principal

If the teacher gets along well with others but doesn't have a grasp of instruction,

- Assign specific tasks for the mentor.
- Because the teacher appears to get along with others, she may take the mentor's suggestions seriously. Meet with both mentor and teacher to develop a systematic plan for improvement.
- Ultimately, you may need to dismiss the teacher at the end of the year or suggest the teacher transfer. (Unless the teacher is beyond repair, often a transfer to another school where the entire curriculum is program centered with scripted teacher's manuals is a viable option.)

The Ineffective Mental Dinosaur

If the teacher seems popular and has a strong power base among the many veteran teachers,

- Be careful. This is the person who can undermine your hard work if they perceive they are being "picked on." Be careful how you approach this teacher—plan every step of your interaction. Did you memorize the contract? Do it now. A tenured teacher will generally know every line and verse and use it against anything you do "to them."

◆ Such a teacher is very confident that his or her way is the way it should be done. The teacher makes it clear that he or she has nothing more to learn. Is this person highly vocal about what he or she knows or just wants to be left alone?

◆ Either way, individual discussions may help determine whether the teacher is able to add to the progress of the school. If he or she can become part of the solution, great! If not, then you have other choices:

  • Count the number of days until the teacher's retirement and leave him or her alone.

  • Encourage the teacher to consider moving to a school where he or she would be happier (and so would you).

  • Nag the teacher about the things that you expect to change, forcing him or her to want to leave.

  • Begin preparing the teacher for a less desirable teaching assignment for the upcoming year (putting the teacher where he or she can do the least damage to students).

  • Physically assign the teacher to a room in the school away from supporters.

  • Start the proceedings for dismissal and pray that you don't have to go this route.

  • Don't give up.

◆ Review your notes from your meeting with your predecessor. What is the history with this teacher? Arrange a meeting with your supervisor to discuss your concerns and ask for advice on how to proceed.

Questions and Answers

Q: Why should teachers bring their set of yearly plans to the preconference and then again at the time of formal observation?

A: Asking for lesson plans during the preconference accomplishes three things:

  1. It emphasizes the importance you place on teacher planning.

2. It gives teachers a heads up that you will be reading them.

3. As you look at the plans, it gives the teacher a chance to answer any questions that you have about areas of the plans you don't understand. By now, you have reviewed the plans during your drop-in visits and probably have specific questions.

You may be amazed at the number of excuses teachers offer for not bringing the lesson plans to the preconference. The most frequent—always blame technology. "I can't get them off my computer," "My printer broke," or "My home computer isn't compatible with the school computer." In this way, you can get the excuses behind you and start your expectations that you expect the plans available at all times, including during your observation.

Then, during your formal observation, stay long enough to read the plans. It is well worth your time. A struggling teacher usually will not be well organized. The plans tell you whether the teacher is winging it through the lessons. The dog-and-pony show of the observation may or may not reflect instruction during every other day. Find out.

Q: If a teacher is better in one area than another, what is more important, positive interaction or effective instructional practices?

A: In an era when collaboration is key to successful schools, both areas are equally important. Examine your own philosophy. Would you be willing to keep a teacher on the staff who will not contribute to the overall growth and improvement of the school because they appear to have instructional skills? Or would you be willing to keep a teacher on the staff who is popular because he or she is "so nice" but is an ineffective teacher? The challenge occurs when trying to find specific examples of the former without implicating the teacher's teammates. Options were given earlier in this chapter.

Q: If I have an assistant, especially one who has been at the school for a while, why should I meet with him or her after every one of their formal observations?

A: First, you want a complete understanding of how every staff member accomplishes their goals and to what degree. You want first-hand knowledge and specific details based on accurate assessment. You will orchestrate support for each staff member, so you need to know what you are talking about. Also, the assistant principal turnover is getting faster and faster. You don't want an assistant to leave in the middle of the year without knowing what conclusions he or she reached about their assigned observations.

Survival Tips

At least 50% of your time must be in classrooms, drop-in visits, and observations.

Establish a precedent from the beginning that you will consistently spend time in classrooms, interacting with students and staff during the entire year.

Read again last year's assessments and evaluations of each teacher. Is there a discrepancy between your assessment of the teacher and your predecessor's view? What did your predecessor say on the teacher's last evaluation? If you do not agree with the previous year's assessment, then proceed cautiously. If the difference is dramatic, seek advice from the experts on what to say. A teacher who received outstanding evaluations from your predecessor will need a careful explanation concerning the dramatic change in their performance from your perspective. Don't back off, just know what you are doing.

Keep to your exact time schedule for the observation. Nothing frustrates teachers more than planning for the observation, and then you don't show up. Whatever it takes for you to remember, figure it out. At the very least, tell teachers to call the office to locate you if you are not in their classroom on time. Teachers still are trying to figure out their level of trust. They will be more forgiving after you have been with them for a few years.

"C minus" teachers are the most difficult to assess in an honest way. Often, their previous assessments and comments are so generic you cannot figure out what to do, especially if you think they are not up to your standards.

Seek the advice from the formal support system that exists, such as the district Human Relations Department. Learn from them how to couch your words to make your point while not overdoing it. You are not able to make a decision this early in the year about what you plan to do about this teacher, but give yourself some wiggle room. Stick with the facts as you assess. At the very least, you will need to place them on an informal improvement plan.

Expect every teacher to make lesson plans and student assessments—both formal end-of- unit tests and other authentic assessments, including student portfolios (if there are any)—available to you whenever you come into the classroom.

- Teachers who are at risk often have lesson plans you can't follow and student assessments that do not reflect consistent evaluation of student work.

- Collect lesson plans from individuals for a specific purpose as a precursor to an individual conference. This is smart and efficient.

- Often, principals collect lesson plans, make comments, and return them weekly. This is an enormous amount of work. Instead, consider reading lesson plans each time you make a visit to the classroom. In this way, you can match the plans with the instruction as it occurs. Then, immediate feedback is possible.

- The exception is when providing lesson plans to you or your assistant on a weekly basis becomes part of an improvement plan for a struggling teacher, and you use this method to monitor progress of the individual teacher's planning.

What if you get advice from your supervisor that says you will keep the dinosaur in spite of your concerns? Sometimes it isn't worth the time and effort to document tenured teachers for removal when others before you would not, unless they have done something so illegal that it is a nonissue. However, if the issue is one of ineffective teaching and you will not get support for your decision, then get creative and let it go. Figure out an assignment for the teacher in which he or she can do the least harm to the fewest number of children. (Unfortunately, during these high-stakes times, that position if very difficult to find.)

Ask your mentor and supervisor for advice. Spending 90% of your time on 10% of the people who don't care that "the book" exists is an enormous frustration and a waste of time in the long run. Don't "die on this hill."

Before making the decision to dismiss a tenured teacher, estimate the teacher's power base. Proceed accordingly. If there is a very strong power base and you risk the chance of a challenge from the teacher's union or a large group that supports the teacher, receive as much help from experts as possible.

When you spend extra time in the teacher's classroom, as you will when verifying your decision, the rumors will begin to fly. Teachers tend to gossip a lot when another teacher appears to be at risk. Recognize that this is the reality and plan methodically. Don't give up.

The message becomes clear. You won't be intimidated by a crabby, vocal teacher. Your expectations about effective teaching are consistent across the board. No one person is held harmless.

Dismissing or not reappointing a teacher is a difficult decision, but doing nothing is worse than doing something.

- You are building a staff that you can work with and that will help you implement your vision.
- Assess teachers who don't get along with their team very carefully. It is harder to document but damaging to the progress of your vision. The teacher needs to know what is occurring. It is not uncommon for the teacher to "not get it." This is the type who will frequently say that "no one ever told me." Their teammates may not have confronted such a teacher, they just talk to each other. You are expected to talk to the teacher—that's the reason you get paid the "big bucks."
- If you know a teacher won't work out, let him or her go. This is the one who might work somewhere else more effectively.

When you have a "lame duck" teacher who is leaving at the end of the year—but that is two months away—say to the teacher, "I realize you are leaving at the end of the year. When you apply for your next position, the principal will call and ask me for a recommendation. What I say to him or her will also include how you perform from now until the rest of the year."

Summary

The importance of accurate and consistent assessments of teachers becomes evident only when principals spend time interacting with teachers. Effective principals watch teachers in classrooms with a specific purpose to provide meaningful feedback concerning the observation.

You conscientiously learn areas of unfamiliar curriculum, instruction, and assessment by watching master teachers work their magic in classrooms. You study and learn from those around you. In his book Learning by Heart, Roland Barth stated, "Learning from experience is not inevitable. It must be intentional" (2001, p. 65).

In this way, you know what you are talking about when you provide meaningful feedback to teachers. You examine organizational strategies through lesson plans and documentation of continuous assessment of student work. You watch interactive instruction between the teacher and students. You know what good teaching should look like in every classroom.

You then engage in thoughtful discussions with teachers. Barth adds, "A precondition for generating 'craft knowledge' is that we must reflect on practice, and find meaning in it" (2001).

Principals ask hard questions of teachers about their instructional and assessment practices, both to learn from the masters and to assess the novices. Questions include, "Explain why you did it that way," "How do you know students learn what you teach?" and "How is your instruction consistent with the school's philosophy?"

Principals ask hard questions of themselves: "How can I learn more about the areas where I lack experience?" "How can I support teachers in better ways?"

You know that decisions regarding the appointment or dismissal of teachers require methodical analysis of all the documentation. That documentation begins during the first weeks of school.

Reflections

1. It is easier to adhere to a drop-in visit schedule during the first two months. But as the year goes on, the schedule is harder to maintain. As a principal, what strategies could you use to ensure that classroom visitations are your highest priority throughout the year?

2. You visit the classroom of a first-year teacher; this is your second visit. You cannot figure out what the teacher is doing. You sit down and look over the lesson plans. It is hard to make the connection between the plans and the observed instruction. What would you do?

3. Your predecessor gave a third-year teacher satisfactory evaluations. At the end of this year, the teacher could be recommended for tenured status. After the first formal evaluation, you conclude the teacher is not that strong. What are the strategies you would put in place?

4. You find out from another teacher that one of the mental dinosaurs bad-mouthed you to other members of the faculty after you made a drop-in visit to her classroom. She thinks you stayed longer in her classroom than in other classrooms you visited, and she will probably call the union to complain. What are your options? Specifically, what would you do?

5. Explain in detail the areas of the curriculum in your school in which you have limited background, such as media, art, music,

physical education, vocational education, or technology. How will you effectively observe teachers in those areas?

6. Assume that you came into administration with a background that is not in the classroom, such as kindergarten through Grade 5 or 6; content areas such as math, social studies, science, language arts, or exceptional education; or English for speakers of other languages. Review how you would effectively observe teachers in those areas. Describe your strategies for observation to provide teachers with meaningful feedback.

8

Utilizing Data and Standardized Testing to Make Decisions: The Testing Plan—Stakes Are high, but It Is Not My Fault, Yet!

(Winter Break)

Every district across the country approaches standardized testing in different ways. Some place more emphasis than others. This chapter provides a perspective based on school districts that accentuate state and national testing of students.

Time spent with your buddy allows you to blow off steam regarding the issues surrounding state standardized testing and the No Child Left Behind mandates. Whatever pressure exists in your school district, it is what it is. You are living in an era of serious accountability. Solutions come from your ability to analyze, solve problems, and draw informed conclusions (Sergiovanni,

1999) based on existing data that tell a story about student progress in your school.

Unless you have memorized all components of the last two year's test scores, it's time to go over them again. By now, you are probably asking yourself, "Just how many times do I have to look at the test data?" Actually, as often as it takes for you to have a clear understanding of all the complexities of each student's performance on the standardized tests. Information you discover in the investigation will have greater implications for all areas of curriculum, instruction, and assessment in your school (Tucker & Stronge, 2005).

The good news is that you are becoming more familiar with the culture and dynamics of the school. Each time you look at the information, you narrow the focus and make different connections. The pieces should begin to fall into place. You began studying the test scores in Chapter 2, before you understood the school culture.

However, so many other issues fell onto your plate that, unless you were careful, what you thought you had figured out during the first go-around of examining student progress may have gone onto the back burner. As you look at your calendar, it is not surprising that time is evaporating. Here is what you have studied:

- The first time, before school began, you saw a *global view* of the school's performance. This provided you with an overview of all students and where the school currently ranks.

- The next time, you looked at *grade-level* and *departmental* scores. Are students, as a whole, showing adequate progress within the grade and department?

- Then you reviewed test results from the perspective of *individual teachers*. Is there any significant difference in the improvement of students when comparing teachers within the same grade level and department? Why?

- *Individual student* scores will be evaluated next. You are looking for individual improvement for each student.

- Next, you will wrap your arms around any *programs* or *models* that your predecessor put in place. The data will give you the "what" part of the testing emphasis. Programs, models, and instructional strategies become the "how."

This is when you finally begin to connect the dots as you begin to determine the whys and wherefores of past practices, quantitative results, and the effect of those components on individual student progress. Your thorough understanding and recall concerning test scores also provides the credibility you need when discussing existing issues and future considerations for the improvement of student learning with teachers and parents.

When Do I Begin?

Although there is a continuous emphasis on effective instruction, generally issues of the upcoming tests become intensified in January. Each school is unique in its approach. If the pressure on you is high, then you probably will use the following information earlier in the year. It is your call. Depending on the school district, the emphasis on standardized testing might begin the day the school door opens and doesn't stop until the last pencil has dropped (or the last student—whichever comes first).

There are two specific issues regarding testing: First, good instruction occurs when students are taught foundational skills that lead to problem solving and critical and higher-level thinking (Kohn, 1998). Students with those skills are generally good test takers. Second, there are specific testing strategies that help all students when that testing day comes. That means that if you choose January as your time to zero in on standardized testing issues, you have less than three months to influence teacher instruction and student performance on "the tests" (assuming that testing occurs in March).

What Should I Do and How Should I Do It?

Your chances of affecting testing results during your first few months on the job are minimal. You are still sorting out all the details on how things came into being—keep digging. The following questions may help you to think of your next steps. You can still assist teachers during the testing phase at the school.

- ◆ How are human resources used to improve test scores?
  - How soon did teachers receive the names of students who have adequate testing data that indicate they did not progress according to the rate expected?
  - Did teams and mentors discuss those individual students and provide strategies to help the student and teachers?
  - Were any staff members moved from one position to another for the purpose of assisting low- or high-performing students? If not, why not?

- Were any staff members moved from one position to another because they experienced consistent low performance from students? Where were they assigned? If a low-performing teacher was not reassigned, why not?

- Were new teachers assigned to a specific group of students or a particular program because of test results? If not, why not? What is the program? On what basis were the students selected for the program? Why was this particular program chosen? (What did your predecessor say? What did the Leadership Team say?) What is different about this program compared to a regular classroom in terms of instructional strategies and expected outcomes? As you talked to the new teachers, looked at student assessments, and observed the students in class, what is your assumption about the effectiveness of the program?

◆ What financial resources are provided to increase test scores?

- Did the school receive any additional funding to support programs for students who did not improve at a satisfactory level?

- If so, how was that money allocated? More staff, more technology, more instructional materials, time and resources for staff development, or more physical space for smaller class sizes?

- Did your predecessor move resources around to accommodate the needs of students with no additional funding, such as increasing some class sizes in advanced classes so that the class sizes for low performing students are lower or eliminating some classes to allow for others?

- Are financial resources obtained through any additional funding? For example, does your school write grants or use money from lease agreements, vending machines, and schoolwide or organization fund-raisers? If so, do any of those monies affect programs that support student achievement? Do you agree with those decisions? If not, do not jump to any specific conclusions yet. Continue to study the student data.

Planning Meeting with the Leadership Team: Testing Focus

Now that you have answered questions that surround testing issues (and thought of a lot more that you included), it is time for the Leadership Team to meet again. The Leadership Team can be very helpful as you get a reality check on your findings. You still don't have all the answers, nor should you feel that you should. Get some help. Word will spread that you want to involve others in the decision-making process (Maxwell, 1995). That is a good thing.

The most productive use of time occurs when key players in leadership roles meet for a full day. In this way, you can focus when discussing issues, drawing conclusions, and developing plans.

You and your team may believe that additional time is needed later for specific teachers (usually the new ones) to meet together. This costs money for substitutes. You will need to find the money.

If you can't find any money at all, then you will have to be satisfied with asking people to meet with you after school. This isn't the most productive use of time because everyone is tired at the end of the day, but it is better than not bringing your team together to help you.

Provide your Leadership Team with enough time to discuss issues with you that will result in a plan to focus on upcoming testing. A full day of planning away from the students and your undivided time are smart ways to examine current testing practices and strategies to support teachers. Your team has a pulse on the school, and this is an efficient use of your time.

Support for New Teachers

Although you probably provided new teachers with help at the beginning of the year, when it comes to issues relating to testing, test-taking strategies, and testing protocol, you might be amazed at how much went in one ear and out the other. It may seem expensive to hire substitutes for a day, but there are several reasons why this will help new teachers at a time of the year when they need extra support.

- Some schools grow so quickly as the year progresses that it becomes necessary to divide classes as new ones are added after school begins. These teachers did not have the benefit of any prior discussions concerning testing issues. They need a lot of help.

- Most schools assign a mentor for every new teacher. However, that does not guarantee that each mentor will deliver the same testing messages to their mentoree. New teachers need to hear the same information and strategies for preparing students for the test.

- Even if there were preliminary discussions with new teachers, they are so overwhelmed with all of their new responsibilities that, unless they have a master teacher who is attached at the hip as their mentor and coach , then new teachers need a day to focus. Testing issues are usually foreign to the novice.

♦ A teacher who enters the school after everyone else has settled in usually receives little or no support. Once school begins, teachers are so busy that it is hard for them to take time to bring someone else up to speed. A specific plan needs to be addressed during the Leadership Team meeting to meet the needs of teachers hired after school begins.

How can you provide efficient and smart support to teachers? The following questions can generate a few ideas for your Leadership Team meeting:

♦ What can we do from January until the test to support our new teachers?

• How many instructional days are left?

• What support can we provide our new teachers so they will realistically approach their subject areas and test preparation in the time that remains?

• If we provide a day for all new teachers to work together away from the students and identify reasonable expectations for pacing and testing strategies, who would lead the meeting? Should the mentors attend with those they mentor?

• We can identify each student in the teacher's classroom who did not make adequate improvement over the last two years. What additional support can we give teachers to help with each of those identified students?

♦ During this meeting, identify how the team, department, or grade-level leaders intend to discuss upcoming testing ideas and issues, including the following:

• What strategies do you intend to use for those students who not only are below expectation but also those who are bright enough but aren't making the improvement they should?

Where Does the Time Go?

An additional discussion for the Leadership Team relates to the importance of using every available moment for instruction. When examining existing practices to prepare students for the test, one frequent discussion point emerges. Where will teachers find the time to teach both the instructional pieces of the test, such as how to think about the content, and still include test-taking strategies?

Where does the time go? There are three issues regarding the imposed lack of instructional time:

1. The school district chips away at learning time.
2. The individual school creates events and activities that disrupt instructional time. These were identified on the calendar you created in Chapter 1.
3. Individual teachers eat away at student learning time.

All of these areas affect student opportunities to receive planned teacher instruction. This information is revealed through individual lesson plans; check that part out the next time you stop into a classroom.

The elusive time issue can extend beyond the number of days, such as those you identified on the calendar, to finding minutes in each day and should become a part of the Leadership Team discussion. The Leadership Team will help determine the best way to solve the time issues.

Time Sensitivity for Students

Create suggestions for teachers to assign tasks based on the number of minutes that the standardized test requires. Students frequently struggle with the timing constraints during the test because they do not have a built-in clock. What does one minute feel like? For example, students can be asked to complete a math problem-solving experience in three minutes.

Younger students tend to rush because they have no internal clock. They hurry because someone finished before them. They think they "won't be first" or that they are "running out of time." Older students may spend too much time on each item. They are more aware of what it takes to receive the highest score, so they may tend to overperfect a piece of work. And unfortunately, there is the group that gets discouraged. They believe they don't get it and "fake" focusing on the test. They watch out of the corners of their eyes to pace their answers at about the same rate as everyone else without understanding what to answer, so they guess randomly. Or, as one teacher observed, the student answered the test items by using the strategy of sequencing his selection by saying to himself, "eanie, meanie, miny, mo; eanie, meanie, miny, mo ..." (eanie, A; meanie, B; miny, C; mo, D). Random strategies also include "Christmas treeing."

When identifying the need for students to become time sensitive, standardized test practice should not be given for homework. Writing or math problems that are assigned will need teacher guidance for direct teaching strategies and assistance when learning how to pace their responses to test items. This can occur only in class.

Time Sensitivity for Teachers

How much *transition time* do teachers waste within an instructional block? Earlier chapters discussed the cumulative effect that wasting even five minutes has on instructional time when teachers begin or end their day or class period.

Have teachers discussed the *pacing* of their instruction throughout the year to accommodate strategies and skills that students need before the test? If so, did teachers reach agreement about the success or lack of success when implementing pacing techniques? Do teachers acknowledge that every student won't be ready for every item on the test? Therefore, hitting the highlights of every topic that will be on the test does not ensure the students will be able to understand test questions. Students with limited or no depth of understanding about a concept will not make the transition from the information they heard to the unfamiliar wording of the test item.

Do teachers *overteach*? Are assessments often completed for teachers to verify that students learned the strategies or skills and that they can move on? Do some teachers "beat a dead horse" because every student needs it rather than plan for small-group instruction to reteach those who don't understand, provide enrichment activities for those who understand the concept, and get on with it?

Do teachers *underteach*? Do teachers drag instruction on and on, remaining oblivious to their own instructional pacing? If so, will students become totally unprepared for strategies to approach test items when, developmentally, they were ready for faster-paced instruction? How will you know? Ask the teacher to explain his or her pacing. Check with other members of the team or department to compare pacing strategies. What makes sense?

Do all teachers, including *math, science,* and *social studies* teachers, actively engage in teaching students strategies for reading and writing with an expository format? A large percentage of standardized testing at every level emphasizes expository text and involves topics in science, social studies, and related areas. For example, do math teachers emphasize the skills needed to read and understand the wording of a math item?

An efficient use of teacher and student time places equal responsibility for test preparation relating to the reading portions in the hands of more than just the teachers in the English Department or the reading block. Reading instruction should include content-area genres in an integrated method and extend beyond the use of biographies to teach students how to read expository text within a social studies class.

Is there *continuous and focused instructional time*? Refer again to your calendar in Appendix A. Are events planned that you know will take enormous amounts of teacher and student time that can be eliminated next year? What would it take to convince the teachers and students involved that specific learning time must replace some activity time? For example, some things such as homecoming are institutionalized and will be with you forever. But are there activities within that event that can be eliminated or reduced? Does the pep rally have to take one hour? Can it take 30 minutes instead?

Sometimes a teacher will create an event or activity that seems to have no bearing on real-world learning or entrenched tradition—it is just that the individual teacher "always did it." The teacher has lots of materials to support the activity and does not want to give up all of the accumulated resources. Encourage teachers who will not let go of their treasured instructional topic to teach it during a time (such as just before a holiday break) that is less intrusive on meaningful learning.

Past Practices Interrupt Student Learning

In addition to the interruptions identified on your calendar, past practices also fragment student learning. Testing schedules often drive everything else in the school.

In some middle and high schools, students stay in one room during the testing block of time, which sometimes can involve as much as three hours at a time. That means that all the other students who not taking the standardized tests cannot change classes during that time because they have no place to go. (Add two more days of lost instructional time to the list.)

True Story

I overheard a parent talking to his daughter in a local gift shop. He said, "Honey, what are you doing here. You are supposed to be in school." "No, I'm not, I'm in seventh grade. The eighth-grade kids are taking tests so they sent the sixth- and seventh-grade kids home.' The dad replied, "What are those tests anyway, some kind of airborne disease that you'll catch if you are in school?"

—Parent of a seventh-grade student

At our high school, only about 10 percent of the students who were not taking the standardized tests showed up for school for the last two days. They knew that they would be held hostage in someone's classroom for three hours at a time. Teachers knew the students wouldn't show up, so most of them planned for a study hall kind of day. The kids knew that.

—High school teacher

Teacher Absenteeism

Absenteeism by teachers is damaging to student progress. If a student is making minimal progress, can you track the number of instructional days lost based on either the teacher's or the student's absences? How many days does the district contract allow teachers to take time off from school, in addition to the usual sick leave allowed? Consider the following example of a student who made minimal progress last year as you factor in lost instructional days as a result of teacher and student absences.

Example

Student name: J.C. Smith
Year: 185 instructional days
Teacher absences: 6 days personal leave, 5 days illness
Student absences: 7 days
18 days lost from instruction before subtracting the other lost instructional days (see calendar).
Add on school-related absences: _____
Practice for events _____
Field trips _____
Events and pep rallies _____

It is possible for a student to make up the work he or she lost while being absent. However, an absent teacher means lost instruction.

A teacher's absence at the elementary school level is especially significant because the child loses an entire day of instruction, whereas at the middle and high school level, the student loses the one period.

Factor in lost instruction time under the assumption that teachers will take the maximum amount of time off allowed in their contract. How many days will that take away from direct teacher instruction? Keep in mind that there is little you can do about it, other than bring it to everyone's attention as you add up the time available for instruction.

Students who are affected by more than one of their teacher's frequent absences in one year may exhibit poor performance.

Student Absenteeism

What system is there in place at the school to remain attentive to students with chronic absences? Naturally, student absenteeism is problematic and requires investigation. Additional staff members, such as a guidance counselor or social worker, can help to examine the issues when a chronic problem exists.

Some schools have the technology to call the homes of absentee students, whereas smaller schools may contact each absent student's home for verification of the student illness.

Parent Infringement on Instructional Time

Some parents arrange medical and dental appointments during the school day and remove the student for half or full days, when an after-school appointment is possible. Other parents remove their child from school during the day because the parent has an appointment that will interfere with after-school pick-up time. In some cultures, the entire family attends to the needs of a relative in another country, state, or town for large blocks of time. Work with your teachers and identify strategies to help with parent communication concerning non-illness-related absences.

What's a Principal to Do?

Instructional time lost through teacher absenteeism needs continuous review. Create a system to keep track of teacher attendance. Frequent or prolonged absences because of illness, pregnancy, or injury can be another reason student test scores are not improving. Some school districts include the number of days a teacher was absent for the year as part of the teacher's end-of-year assessment.

Identify options to support students who have fragmented instruction. For example, there are teachers who not only substitute on a day-to-day basis but also those who become a permanent substitute for a teacher's long-term leave during the year. They may have no clue how to teach. Worse yet, it is not uncommon for substitutes to enter classrooms in which no lesson plans exist. They often will grab materials from a neighboring teacher (whether it fits the actual lessons for the students or not) and "student-sit" all day. Often, the principal doesn't realize there were no plans because fellow teachers come to the rescue and don't say anything.

As principal, investigate the quality of work assigned to students when the teacher is absent. A common option for a substitute is to show a video or movie that is unrelated to current instruction and replaces direct instruction with "busy work" to fill the rest of the day. Find out whether the time spent while the substitute works with students maintains or interrupts the flow of instruction.

What are the plans to accommodate the needs of a long-term substitute? For example, if you have a teacher who knows that he or she will be out of school for more than one week, how far in advance will you expect the teacher to complete lesson plans? What arrangements will you make for a teacher who is out on maternity leave and will be absent for two months or more?

During the week or weeks of testing, teachers often perceive that students are too tired to engage in any other academic tasks. Review lesson plans for the testing weeks. Does learning continue even when students are not engaged in formal testing? Why or why not? Who makes that decision? Teachers and students need to understand that you expect continued learning to occur around and beyond the testing schedule.

Early in your principal's role, establish your rules regarding policies you will put into place for student absences and your expectations for parents. This may become a problem if your predecessor did not maintain a formal policy, so be prepared for an early struggle with a newly implemented policy. For example, you want to stop the lax adherence to the rule that students cannot leave campus during the day without an official doctor's appointment notice. Past practices may have made constant exceptions depending on the insistence of the parent or the pleading of a high school student. Only if you do not make an exception will you be able to hang on to this policy. If you cannot enforce a rule, abandon it. Find a compromise. But, remember the goal is to minimize lost instructional time.

Field Trips: Time Compared to Value

Analyze the value of planned field trips. A specific field trip can become an institutionalized event that would be hard, if not impossible, to eliminate. Trips to national monuments or cities are examples. Parents and grandparents may have gone to Washington, DC, to observe the legislative process, and so will their children—you may not want to "die on that hill." Field trips for this year are probably already planned. The physics class always goes to the local amusement park to study roller coasters. Of course, because they are there, they will stay all day. Middle and high school field trips are especially problematic because it takes the entire day away from other classes.

Elementary teachers can more easily integrate their learning into all subject areas. However, a trip to the library that also includes a picnic in the park and a dodgeball game needs clarification concerning learning objectives for the whole day.

Because you are the new kid on the block, it is logical that you will inquire about why some field trips are part of the curriculum. Be careful of a rationale that does not make sense. The question is, is it worth the time and effort compared to the value of learning?

There are specific things that you can ask:

- Will students know and understand more about the concept being taught as a result of this experience? How will you know?
- What instruction will precede the trip?
- Why was this particular field trip selected?
- How many chaperones are needed?
- How will the costs be covered?
- Is there a copy of the trip agenda for you?
- What is the time frame for each activity when the students arrive at their destination?
- What is the departure time from school and the return arrival time? How much total instruction time will be lost from other classes?
- What follow-up assessment will be used after students return to school?

As a compromise for next year, consider moving the time for the field trips for grades affected by the assessments until after testing time, unless the content of the trip correlates directly with upcoming tests. Could an outside expert come into the classroom and provide the same information and experience for the students?

At the completion of the Leadership Team meeting, a plan will emerge to focus on ways to help the new teacher, as well as ways to help teachers understand the importance of time utilization and testing preparation. Finally, the Leadership Team should understand your position on testing so that they will share your beliefs with their team members. This is additional support for you.

As the following section indicates, you may want to change some of the testing traditions. Teachers need to hear your rationale, not only from you but also from their teammates.

What Can the Principal Do about the Upcoming Tests?

Even though you have minimal control over the upcoming test results, there are things that many principals do to help parents and teachers understand the importance of doing well on the test. One recommendation that some principals promote include is to have the cafeteria provide high-protein breakfasts and lunches (some schools offer them free to everyone on testing days). Students are expected to bring high-protein snacks and water, or teachers should provide peanut butter and crackers on testing days for students in need.

True Story: Teacher's Bulletin

> Don't forget that your classrooms should provide a cinnamon fragrance in the room and peppermint candy to students (unless they cannot have sugar) to produce brain stimulation and help students focus. Students should enter the room that is dimmed and has quiet Renaissance music, preferably by Brahms or Beethoven, playing in the background to calm students before testing begins.
>
> —A middle school principal

You undoubtedly have read about unique methods, strategies, remedies, and theories concerning what it takes for students to perform well on tests. You will carefully observe and ask questions concerning current practices and determine which, if any, you will promote in the future. In truth, you know that students perform best when they learn to focus and think critically about the content of the test and test-taking strategies throughout the entire year. (Although what student will turn down a chance to eat candy during class?)

Parents and Testing

There are some ways that you can involve parents in the testing process.

- The first parent conferences should include conversations about the child's progress and the potential for achievement on the standardized tests.
- Provide a parent night for testing information.
  - Parents are provided with sample test items.
  - Teachers and administrators are there to answer questions.
  - Parents actually take the test. (Some parents will not take the test. They will be embarrassed if they don't answer the items correctly.)
  - Parents can learn test-taking strategies.
- Provide parents with fundamental ways to assist their children.
  - Teacher and school newsletters might explain the importance of students eating a nutritious breakfast and getting a good night's sleep every night, including testing days.

True Story

I can't believe it. My mom wakes me 30 minutes early so that I will eat a big breakfast. Do you know what she made me eat—bacon and eggs and orange juice? I hate eggs and the bacon was all greasy. I can't wait for tests to get over so I can go back to my cereal and sleep 30 minutes longer.

—Student complaining to the other,
overheard by a fifth-grade teacher

Public Relations and "The Test"

Just when you determine that you can't think about testing any longer, there is more. So you won't be blindsided, don't be surprised if your supervisor and school community expect you to provide a public relations blitz on behalf of the upcoming test. There are principals who either enjoy the publicity or give in to public pressure to do something "exotic" to promote the upcoming test.

You have read about principals who kiss a pig, dance a jig on the school roof, get "slimed," or become the target on a dunking stool if the students reach a particular testing goal. At the extreme are school communities who offer prizes or raffle tickets to each student who attends school during each testing day for a chance to win something elaborate on the last day. In other schools, "rah-rah" assemblies are held, t-shirts are given away, bands play, or cheerleaders cheer. All kinds of extrinsic awards and recognition may be a part of the culture under the assumption that students will perform better on the standardized test when offered an incentive.

Now, if you are the type of principal who enjoys kissing a pig to promote the test, go forth. Keep in mind that whatever you do will set a precedent. Is this your idea of a tradition to start?

The intense high-stakes pressure can prompt principals to make a desperate attempt to show the school community that they are doing everything humanly possible for students to perform well on the test. This can eat up enormous amounts of time, at what cost? Whatever it is, carefully examine current traditions.

Hold to your comfort level. You may be the principal who won't be kissing a pig. If teachers feel that a cinnamon fragrance in their room during testing time helps students focus, then no harm, no foul. Not everything has to remain the same as it was with your predecessor. Nor is there any need to make a big deal about current testing traditions. This is the time of the year when you begin thinking about your own traditions and approaches to the public relations issues regarding testing. How much emphasis will you place on the importance of the test and for what period of time during the year? What can you do this year?

Questions and Answers

Q: January seems late to be examining programs and models. Why wait until then?

A: Because this is your first year, it will take this long before you can get a handle on what is happening in specific programs. In addition, it usually takes time for teachers to give you objective feedback concerning the progress of the program or model.

There are exceptions. For example, there may be a group of students who are assigned to a program for a short period of time for intense remediation. If the model is based on skill development followed by skill testing, the results will be immediate. If this is the case, assessment of the program or model is easier to quantify, and decisions about the effect on student progress are easier to analyze.

Q: What can I accomplish between now and test time that could make a difference? Testing will occur in March, and that means there are only two months left.

A: You can establish the tone that you want to set for the school in ways such as visiting classrooms to watch how testing strategies are being addressed or, instead of an all-school assembly that eats into instructional time, visiting each classroom of sophomores, eighth graders, and third graders (for example) to emphasize the importance of taking the test seriously and doing well.

One high school principal reminded the students that if they allowed themselves to fall into the bottom two levels on the test, next year, they would not be able to take any electives. Instead, they would be scheduled into remedial reading classes. (Desperate problems result in desperate measures.) If any instructional time is interrupted, it must be cleared through you, the principal.

Q: What if it appears that a program is not working? It is January, and I am not familiar enough with the program to know what to do next. What should happen?

A: What makes you think the program is not working? Is it the program, the students, the teacher, or a combination? Do you have data from the teacher that causes you concern? Unless this is a self-contained program in which the students are there all day, other teachers are involved. Plan a meeting with the teacher. Is it the teacher? Then bring in teachers who also serve the same students. If the problem is the student, then others will have similar concerns. Other teachers may provide insight into a combination of the student and the program. Take minutes of these meetings because you will need them later as you evaluate individual student needs, individual teachers, and program assessments.

Q: Teacher absenteeism is beyond my control. What can I do about it?

A: There are a few ideas that can help you become more proactive regarding teacher absences.

- Review your substitute bank. Large districts often use a computer-generated substitute system, and you could get anybody. However, most schools have identified a group of substitutes that are fairly effective.

- When a teacher is absent, make a concerned inquiry about the reason. It establishes good rapport with the teacher and gives you additional insight concerning the teacher's absence. Mention the lesson plans made available and applaud the good ones.

- Conscientiously review teacher's substitute lesson plans. Visit the classrooms of substitute teachers. Look at the lesson plans available. Did the teacher provide quality instruction? Did the other team members provide their plans for the substitute?

- Word gets around quickly if you check substitute plans. It is an important part of your assessment of the teacher.

Q: I assume that by assigning a mentor and coach to a new teacher, the mentor will assist him or her with testing issues. What else can I do?

A: This is not an assumption to make.

- Begin with a meeting in which you personally introduce the mentor and coach to the mentoree.

- Discuss your expectations for them both.

- Establish a system for new teachers that includes a checklist of everything they need or where to find information concerning any upcoming standardized testing.

- Establish a checklist within each grade level, department, or team that provides established practices, such as how test practice is conducted, where the testing resources are located, what to do with them, and the testing protocol.

- Identify the difference between a mentor and a coach. A mentor might provide a teacher with the "warm fuzzies" needed to maintain sanity. A coach gives strategies for curriculum, instruction, and assessment. Each new teacher needs a coach.

 ## Survival Tips

Don't bend to political pressure that you inherited and move out of your comfort level to improve test scores through a personal performance. Follow the logic of student testing performance. Ask yourself, "What research supports the use of extrinsic rewards as a way for students to improve test scores?" Before you draw your line in the sand, ask your supervisor about his or her expectations concerning the traditions you want to change.

Is it important to "kiss a pig," unless you think students will learn more effectively as a result? If you enjoy doing dramatic things to entertain the students, do it during such events as the family carnival day. It is important to become a part of the community and its expectations; however, you can be visible in many ways of your choosing.

Be aware of the unwritten ways teachers support student-wasted time. You won't find it in lesson plans, and, unless you observe the task during classroom visits, you will miss it. But try this: Stand by the copy machine and look at what teachers want copied. You will quickly determine the quality of thinking required by teachers. Notice the pages where fill-in-the-blank, commercially generated pages require only low-level thinking. In teacher conferences, examples of copied work is a specific way to show student-wasted time.

True Story

I couldn't believe that teachers request Word Search pages copied for the students. The students love them because it is a no-brainer; teachers seem to like them because it keeps the kids quiet. Give me a break! Where in the real world will students see words written all in capital letters, vertically, and diagonally? Crossword puzzles I could live with for the last hour before the holiday break—just to keep kids from climbing the walls, but Word Search? Teachers laughed when I brought it to their attention. I guess they didn't want to think about the purpose.

—Middle school principal

Student projects—does the end justify the means? Examine student projects that demonstrate a culminating learning experience. Ask the student and, finally, the teacher, "Explain the purpose of this project. What specific learning occurred?"

Did the student complete the project entirely at school? How much instructional time was used to create the project? Could the same learning have occurred in any less time-intensive way?

Naturally, there are some classes in which a product is the learning, such as in art, music, drafting, robotics, technology, and vocational classes. However, in most circumstances, those products are also guided by the teacher as the student proceeds through to the finished work. Learning is not just about "doing something."

True Story

> Our middle school gymnasium was converted to give the appearance of an underwater environment because the students were studying an ecology unit. It took the students about two weeks to hang the ceiling and walls with blue-died material. Couldn't the time have been used more effectively? The teacher was into the project before I realized the extent of the project. I really let that one slip by, and at what cost to higher-order thinking?
>
> —Middle school principal
>
> The students were studying Native American Indian cultures. They were to recreate the homes where a tribe of their choice lived. It was a project for homework. They were displayed in the media center. It was so obvious—the elaborate ones that the parents and child created, compared to the little construction paper teepee that drooped at an angle. What was learned, and by whom?
>
> —Elementary school principal

Identify teachers who may begin teaching after the school year begins. They need strong support, yet they are often the forgotten ones. you and the faculty are so busy once school starts that the teacher who enters late is often inadvertently neglected. A mentoring and support system is needed to help bring the teacher up to speed. The teacher is especially handicapped if he or she is teaching the classes affected by the tests. More difficult is the teacher who has no experience.

Substitute teachers create a challenge. Often, there are few good ones. The issues addressing long-term substitutes are the same as those for hiring new teachers after school starts. Provide any newly hired teacher with the same support. Lost meaningful learning time can affect student performance, and a methodical plan that involves mentoring, coaching, and monitoring must go into place immediately.

Many parents are more aware than ever when student learning is interrupted because of a change in teachers. You are lucky. When parents are concerned, they are interested. One strategy is that as soon as you believe that a class is reaching capacity and you might change the student's assignment, become proactive. Provide a parent letter to each new student enrolling after the day that you realize the addition of another class is inevitable. Make of copy of this notification. It is amazing how many parents have selective memory loss when you need to make the change and their response is, "You never told me this would happen."

To the parents of _____,

At this time, your child's class in _____ is
reaching maximum capacity. We may need to change your child's assignment
if an additional class is added. If that occurs, you will be notified prior to the
schedule adjustment.

Date :_____

Parent signature: _____

If I know a teacher will leave during the school year, should parents be notified ahead of time?

- It depends on how much time you want parents fussing at you and students (particularly the young ones) unnecessarily distracted. An expecting teacher usually waits until she is comfortable announcing the upcoming event.
- Whatever the reason, wait as long as possible. It is especially helpful if you can announce the upcoming absence and, at the same time, tell the parents and students about the replacement. This isn't always possible.
- Two letters should go out at the same time, if at all possible: a letter from the teacher who is leaving that provides details

concerning his or her return and a letter from the incoming teacher with an introduction.

Summary

During the first year, you are still identifying the key components of student success—or lack thereof—regarding standardized testing. You can claim that whatever progress students make during your first year is the result of past practices. However, you need a complete and analytical assessment of what currently exists in the school. Total accountability for the school becomes yours very quickly.

In Chapter 1, you studied the test scores from the last two years. However, by this time of the year, you will reexamine the same information with another level of understanding.

The high-stakes testing environment requires methodical and thorough analysis of all components of curriculum, instruction, and assessment and the effect that each has on student progress. This is a complex process because it involves evaluating issues on several levels: the total school ranking; each teacher's progress with his or her class; individual student scores; and individual student progress from one year to the next. Then, to determine the potential effect that specific programs or particular models have on student learning, you will need to learn the rationale and process for the selection of such programs or models.

Time becomes an important factor when analyzing ways to provide teachers with more instructional minutes. You can begin discussions with the faculty on how to find more learning time. This discussion can help teachers from January until testing time. Both teacher and student absenteeism should be included in the conversation and factored into the overall assessment of student progress. If it is a problem, this topic is one that you may wish to add to your "ideas for next year"—keep staff and students in attendance.

Given the enormous pressure in most districts, you need your ducks in a row to identify what happened during your first year, what the results were, and what are your conclusions. When your supervisor asks you to explain the approaches, strategies, and results of the tests for this year, you will have a well-documented explanation. Your job is to improve student learning within an environment that promotes the application and understanding of concepts. Next year is coming all too soon.

Reflections

1. What are some logical approaches to promoting focused attention on how best to improve student's ability to think, solve problems, and work collaboratively as a way to improve standardized test scores?

2. Carefully analyze the methods, approaches, and issues that the school places on the application of student learning on standardized testing. What are they? What can the school community do? What can the teachers do? What can the principal do?

3. List the available staff members who can assist in analyzing last year's test score data from all perspectives: the total school, the individual teachers, individual students who do not receive special support and their teachers, specific programs purchased to support low-performing students, and any additional interventions the school has identified. Identify a strategy that will provide you with the process to receive and use the data effectively.

4. Teachers will need the data on their individual students. How can you facilitate the process of using the information to drive instructional strategies and practices?

5. Collect the data for your individual school. What specific issues emerged from your findings that may cause you to change past practices for next year? What are the issues, and what plan would you put in place to accommodate the needs of teachers and students? What would you add? What would you take away? Why?

6. Identify a program that was purchased to improve test scores. How can you determine the success of the program?

7. As principal, what would you do to reinforce the importance of maximum achievement on the standardized test with two months remaining before the test?

8. Bring your school schedule to a discussion group and combine it into a complete calendar for the year, including the number of days between the beginning of the year and standardized testing. Add all activities that cut into instructional time, such as assemblies and special events. Include the actual number of minutes involved from the time that students are dismissed until they return to class for each identified activity. Total the minutes for the year and determine how many days will be missed. How might this information influence decisions about which activities are worth the time and which are not?

9. Describe the reasons why students lose focused instruction time. Explain the effect of lost instructional time on students. Track two students over the last two years only from the perspective of lost instructional time because of all of the possibilities you described. What conclusions can you draw? What would you do about it?

9

School Improvement Plans, Staff Evaluations, Budgets and Master Schedules: The Final Stretch

(Second Semester)

If you followed the chapters and the sequence of events that have evolved throughout the year, you have accomplished complex tasks and engaged in a complicated fact-finding mission. You have ownership in the school because you are learning the culture, interacting with staff, developing a collaborative environment, and finding your leaders. You are getting to know the school community and identifying issues and concerns that must be addressed from your personal perspective.

Somewhere around the winter break and January, you organized your files of notes taken from your meetings early in the year with those who know the workings of the school and your observations of teachers. You studied them so that you have a clear sense of what makes the school tick.

You then spent time in serious reflection as you explored your inner self to understand your purpose, determined where you are philosophically, and examined your vision. At the early stages of your appointment, you put your position in writing so that you could clarify your own thinking.

Because you now have a better sense of the big picture, you should review and, if necessary, adjust your purpose, philosophy, and vision as they relate to the school. As a principal or assistant principal, this one critical step in defining the foundation on which you will facilitate the improvement of the school is often overlooked or underplayed in the hectic schedule of your days. Rewrite or create the following three key indicators of what you expect of yourself and, ultimately, what you expect of those you work with.

Key Statements that Define Your Core Beliefs (Revised)

Your purpose drives your philosophy, which drives your vision. All remain consistent with each other. They define your passions.

My purpose is _____.

This statement should reflect your fundamental beliefs about your role, not only in your life but also in your life as it relates to your leadership of those around you. Purpose-driven leaders are described in Robert Greenleaf's work surrounding "servant leadership" in the book Reflections on Leadership: How Robert K. Greenleaf's Theory of Servant-Leadership Influenced Today's Top Management Thinkers (Robert Greenleaf Center for Servant-Leadership, 1995).

My philosophy is _____.

This statement is the umbrella belief that explains your combined convictions concerning all stakeholders in your school, with the focus on students. Your philosophical position will drive your vision.

My vision is _____.

This statement identifies the smaller pieces of your philosophy: What do you want to happen for the students, staff, and parents of the school in one-, two-, three-year increments?

This statement represents *how* you think you could reach your philosophical position while maintaining your sense of purpose.

This is the purpose that drove the philosophy that became the vision. So this is the "house that Jack built." Both Greenleaf's (1995) servant leadership and Sergiovanni's (1999) transformational leadership describe the importance of purpose, philosophy, and vision when defining the foundational beliefs that are necessary for a leader's long-term success.

Specific clarification of your core beliefs provides a critical lens through which you will proceed during the years at your new school. Write the statements in a place where you will see them as you observe teachers, work with the Leadership Team, facilitate the School Improvement Plan, and make decisions for next year.

Your written beliefs will help you to focus on where you are in relation to the rest of the stakeholders. This is not the time to make your specific statements public; rather, they will guide you in your evaluation of the tasks facing you. Very soon, you will make your vision public. Hang on for the time being.

School districts follow slightly different timelines for the next series of events. The specific issues may vary from district to district, but each of the tasks and situations is consistent, even if the order is different. As a result, the months from January through May are outlined within this chapter. Each area will be identified according to the same structure as the previous chapters.

Continue to examine the monthly tickler file. This will alleviate the need to reinvent details of past practices for institutionalized events. Unless you see some glaring obstacles, let tradition remain and evaluate the situation. You can change or modify past practices next year. Just keep careful notes so that next year, you will remember your observations and make adjustments.

When Do I Begin?

The time frame identified here is based on the tasks and issues that are addressed right after winter break. You may need to adjust the time frame if your district's dates do not coincide.

January is a good time to bring together your School Improvement Planning Team. It is right after winter break, before standardized testing mania, and the staff members are more rested.

During *February and March,* revisit your personal philosophy and vision and facilitate the School Improvement Planning process before more effectively observing the staff for your final observation.

March and April is generally budget time. Budgets are based primarily on staffing needs, with additional money allocated for the basics necessary to run the school. Often, testing weeks occur during these two months and require a set of strategies to keep the staff from getting unusually cranky and the students focused, not stressed.

April, May, and June are often the months when teachers find out about their reappointments. This is also the time that many teachers and students believe that once testing is over, so is focused, direct instruction. End-of-year events and activities can seriously affect learning. This is the time when, in spite of your busy schedule, your position remains one of visibility and observations.

May is generally the time when summer school decisions are made. Staff and students are selected and programs clarified for content. End-of- year events will eat enormous chunks of your time.

Test scores may now be available. That will set in motion a series of events from basic analysis to individual decisions regarding student placement for the upcoming year. Parent meetings often accompany this busy time of the year as decisions regarding students occur.

What Should I Do and How Should I Do It?

January

School Improvement Plan

School districts and states use different titles to describe the planning process and product for the upcoming school year. For the purpose of consistency in this chapter and others, the term "school improvement" denotes any process and concluding decisions used by districts to establish a philosophy, vision, goals, objectives, and timelines to accomplish the desired outcome for a school. Some preliminary work must precede the School Improvement Planning Team meeting.

Each school district maintains a different system or approach to a school plan for improvement. Although there are specific and nonnegotiable tasks that some districts require, the individual needs of the school require intensive study and planning. Individual school plans succeed because teachers, parents, and students participate and understand the importance of owning the plan (Zmuda, Kuklis, & Kline, 2004).

♦ Identify the members of the School Improvement Planning Team.

- Often, your Leadership Team will recommend members, or you will ask the departments or teams to select representatives. You also will want representatives from the noninstructional staff and your administrative team. Keep the numbers manageable.
- The team represents the entire school community. If parents and students are a part of the process, make sure they represent the whole school, not just a personal or small-group agenda.

◆ Find the money to release staff members who may need substitutes for a day to focus on the plan.

◆ Plan for every detail well in advance.

- The development of the plan is an important process and must be well organized and planned. The planning will go more smoothly if you think through the day and what you want to accomplish, with attention to every detail well in advance.
- Perhaps you sent a survey to the staff and school community members to determine which issues to address. Or, at a staff meeting, you asked small groups to identify issues and concerns.
- Prepare as much pertinent information as possible to present to the team so that they can make informed decisions.
- However you gathered the information, you will consolidate this information so that the members will clearly understand how you identified the problems to solve.
- Each member needs a description of the purpose of the meeting and the intended outcomes.

◆ Identify a problem-solving model you plan to use.

- Organize the process of problem solving carefully and methodically (Shapiro, 2003).
- If you are not familiar with a specific problem-solving model that you like, contact your supervisor or mentor for advice and suggestions of models that have been successful.
- If you have never facilitated a problem-solving group before, either find another principal who has used a process successfully and observe him or her or bring in someone from the district level to help you out. Once you see it working, you will be able to conduct a planning meeting on your own.
- Learn how to avoid becoming bogged down in issues that the school has no control over. This is not the time to solve all the societal problems.

- Decide who will facilitate the meeting.
  - Because this is your first year with your School Improvement Planning Team, you have two choices regarding who should facilitate this meeting: Either you or a member of your team can facilitate.
  - Because you, as principal, will set the tone for the future of the school, it is appropriate for you to run the meeting. After the first year, you may feel that you can turn over the job to someone else (unless you are so uncomfortable with the process and you want to watch someone else serve as the facilitator).
- Appoint someone outside the team to take minutes.
- Gather information concerning programs or models implemented during the last two years.

The rationale for the selection of a new program often exists when a new model might improve test scores and student progress. The questions that were used to identify specific programs are the same questions used to identify the models. What effect is it having on student progress? What effect does it have on teacher instruction? How is student progress measured?

As principal you would ask, "How did we get this program or model in the first place?" When an area is problematic within a school and everyone's best attempts to make the situation better have met with little success, frustration can often override common sense. The result is that programs are sometimes purchased without thoroughly examining the impact the program will have on the existing infrastructure of the school.

Salespeople with a gift for "selling refrigerators to Eskimos" can provide an impressive array of reasons to purchase their program that will cure all ills. They provide documents in fancy binders that display state benchmarks, standards, expectations, assessments, and research. They probably provide food for the teachers to view their wares.

These could take the form of everything from a textbook series, supplemental content materials, or a specific program to pieces of technology. Did your predecessor or department fall prey to a sales pitch that didn't make good on its promises?

In some districts, the decision might be made for you. Orders come from above that state that you will purchase program Z or textbook series Q. (Even district-level specialists can be led astray by promises that offer the moon and the stars and instead produce earth dust.) Unless there is absolutely no choice, wait on any decision that will cost money in time or resources for the purchase of a new program or expensive materials. The decision could affect an entire school (such as the adoption of a math or science program), an individual department (such as the adoption of a new literature series), or a specific program (such as programs that support second-language learners). As you make curriculum decisions, realize that waiting provides you with time to gather adequate information so that when money is spent, it is spent wisely and prudent decisions are made.

- If the program or model involved several teachers, then it saves time if you gather the information from those who implemented the program or model prior to the all-day School Improvement Planning Team meeting.

- You will determine a method to best gather the information. This might include a presentation by those involved or a written report. The audience for these reports could be you, the Leadership Team, team or department leaders, or whomever makes sense. This knowledge will provide the School Improvement Planning Team the needed details when making recommendations concerning how best to serve students for the upcoming year.

Reporting Format for a Program or Model Used in the School

Target students	Program or model	Time	Strategies	Test results	Plan for next year
Bottom 10% of 12th grade	XYZ reading	50 minutes, 5 days all year	Highly structured	80% meeting targets	Add 11th-grade section
Top 15% of 11th-grade English	Honors or AP class	50 minutes, 5 days	AP guidelines	95% meeting targets	Increase to top 20% qualifying
Bottom 10% of 8th-grade math	Tutors	9:00–10:00 every Saturday	Tutor, manual	80% meeting targets	Increase attendance
Bottom 10% of 4th-grade reading	Computer program ABC	Twice per week, computer lab– reading	Program sequence	10% increase in test scores for 70% of students	Move to 3rd grade

Teachers who are directly responsible for implementing a new program or model should be invited to present their assessment of the program, its value, and the progress of the students. A form such as on the previous page may provide suggestions for a method of reporting. In addition, other questions need clarification:

- Why was the specific program identified as filling a need for a particular group of students?
- Is the program or model a total-school initiative, or is it designated for only a specific group of students?
- Does the program appear to work?
- How do you know?
- If the facts support the belief that a program is not working as well as expected, then it is important to discuss what happened.

◆ Determine the time and place for the School Improvement Planning Team meeting.

◆ Create an atmosphere that perpetuates the professional task before the team.

- Organize or delegate the tasks of arranging food, office supplies for each participant, and a token gift (school mug, t-shirt, or whatever the budget or business partners might provide).
- Provide handouts that review the school philosophy and vision, identify the data, and provide any needed background information gathered from surveys or program evaluations.

◆ Identify issues that are not negotiable.

- For example, in the survey, teachers reported that they think program W should be eliminated and the money used for something else. In reality, program W is a federally funded program and cannot be negotiated.
- Compile a list of nonnegotiable items to present to the School Improvement Planning Team. This will save a lot of time.

◆ Make sure your calendar is clear so that you can stay throughout the entire School Improvement Team meeting.

- Unless a life-threatening emergency occurs, do not delegate someone on the staff to act in your absence.
- If you are training an assistant principal, he or she also should remain throughout the meeting to understand the problem-solving process.

The School Improvement Team Meeting

This is the point in time when you begin making your mark on the school while setting the tone that you are part of a collaborative school community. Your ultimate goal is to develop a mutually agreed upon direction for the school that reflects a sound philosophy and vision for the upcoming year.

- You are a member of a team
  - This becomes an interesting balance between the desires of the team and the fact that the implementation of the plan ultimately will rest with you. You have to live with the results.
  - Understand your role in the process. Your team will become advocates for the plan when they have ownership in the outcome.
- Follow the problem-solving model format you selected.
  - Review the philosophy and vision of the school; clarify its meaning.
  - Maintain a list of items on a chart that cannot be resolved during the meeting yet should be acknowledged for resolution at another time. These items are listed either because the issue is unique to the team member or identifies the special interest of one group or because it is too complex to resolve during a singe-day meeting.
  - The problem-solving model should provide a method to identify the issues and determine solutions, timelines, and budgetary considerations.
- Choose only those top issues that you and the staff can realistically accomplish in one year. A three-year plan can evolve from the remaining items.
- Submit the minutes and conclusions to the School Improvement Planning Team for revisions. Write a draft of the plan. Provide the stakeholders with a draft. Recognize that the final plan will not be complete until the standardized test scores become available.
- Provide the final minutes of the meeting to the staff.
- Review the conclusions with the entire staff. Reinforce the importance that this is the school's plan. Your role is to support the teachers in the implementation.

Did you accomplish your goal during the School Improvement Planning process? Did the team leave its time together with a shared commitment to the philosophy and vision of the school? Did you empower all stakeholders?

If so, members of the school community will understand and communicate the school's belief and plan.

Final Observations and Evaluations: February and March

As you work through the final round of observations for the year, you will have more information to support your findings about each staff member. You want staff members who will create a learning environment that is consistent with the school's philosophy and vision. You also have the School Improvement Plan as a basis for determining which individual teachers demonstrate and implement the same common beliefs as the rest of the school. You have watched staff members at work and interacted with them informally and through individual conferences. These are key pieces of your assessment process and your decisions about reappointing those who will enhance the school's progress.

At this time of the year, you will be very grateful for the number of times you visited classrooms, took notes, and conducted teacher conferences. In this way, you can make very informed decisions concerning your recommendations for employment for individual staff members. If you didn't meet your goal of getting into classrooms as often as you had planned, you will begin kicking yourself all around the school.

You have different issues depending on the staff tenure status and any prior plans you established with an ineffective staff member identified earlier in the year. It is very difficult to make decisions concerning the reemployment of teachers when you don't think they are that good. Consider the following questions that principals frequently wrestle with as they begin assessing teachers.

- ◆ What should I do when good, qualified teachers are so hard to find? Should I keep a mediocre teacher rather than hire a brand-new teacher in the hard-to-find areas?

- ◆ If my predecessor gave the teacher good evaluations, but I don't think he or she is that good, then what do I do?

- ◆ The new teacher is really poor. But it is so close to the end of the year; I am simply too tired to go through the hassle of building a case that would prevent her from teaching altogether. I hate to unleash her on an unsuspecting school, but I can't keep her here.

- ◆ I know there are some teachers who are so far off the mark from where the school philosophy and vision will lead us that I won't help the school at all by keeping them here.

Answering these quandaries becomes the hardest part of your job. There are several things to keep in mind.

- Good staff members want capable colleagues. Otherwise, those who are effective, know their jobs, and do them well end up carrying the weight of those who are less competent. Effective teachers want the principal to take a stand with poor teachers.

- Even if staff members know their jobs and appear competent, if they don't get along well with you or other staff members, they will not help you move the school forward.

- If you have a tenured teacher whom you want to move on, get advice from those at the central office and your supervisor as soon as you determine that is your position. Move on it, but move with care and realize this won't happen in one year unless you and the teacher reach a mutual agreement that another school would be in his or her best interest (see Chapter 7).

- When in doubt, put on your parent hat. Is this the teacher whom you would want teaching your child?

- Put on your teacher hat. Is this the teacher with whom you would like to work?

- You already wear your principal hat. Is this a person who will work with you as part of a team to move the school forward?

What are you looking for during your final observations that are different from what you looked for earlier in the year?

- Take the teacher's file with you for the observation. Review your notes from your drop-in visits and the last evaluation. Previous notes and comments become clearer while in the classroom.

- In addition to the district's standard observation form, create specific additional notes to verify your findings (described in Chapter 7).

- What evidence you can identify that shows the teacher used suggestions, ideas, and an understanding of the school's philosophy to improve his or her teaching?

- Your postconference will be a compilation of your observations throughout the year; it must be specific and clearly define the effectiveness of the teacher.

- What evidence do you possess of student progress? (Reeves, 2004)

- Teachers get the message when you provide a lot of information concerning your observation of the teacher's ability. You know what is going on in every classroom.

What information have you compiled on tenured teachers?

- ◆ Often, teaching contracts do not require the same number of observations for tenured staff compared to the newer teachers. This becomes problematic if administrators put tenured staff on the bottom of the list to observe. End-of- year assessments could become a rubber stamp regardless of the competence of the teacher. You will be surprised at the number of teachers who receive their end-of-year assessment without a principal or assistant ever going into the classroom.

- ◆ Information about assessments and what you said to whom spreads quickly. As the new principal, you send a very clear message one way or the other: Either you have a pulse on every classroom or you don't.

What new issues will you discuss with the teachers during the final assessment?

- ◆ You can begin spreading the word about your expectations concerning each staff member's commitment to the philosophy and vision of the school.

- ◆ If you plan to reappoint staff members for next year, you do so because they are demonstrating best practices for students and a collaborative way of working with team members. In addition, the teachers are on the same page as you and the rest of the staff who are being reappointed. As Jim Collins describes in his book *Good to Great*, you will "[g]et the right people on the bus, the wrong people off the bus, and the right people in the right seats" (2001, p. 194).

- ◆ The process of final evaluations and assessments cannot be a rushed process. Your reputation depends on methodical and carefully documented information.

- ◆ The final conference becomes very important.

This is your opportunity to reinforce the philosophy and vision of the school and the importance of the teacher's role in improving student learning. Once again, you can link student assessment, individual student improvement over the year, and teacher evaluations (Tucker & Stronge, 2005).

Testing Time: Surviving March

Between high-stakes testing anxiety, the final round of observations, and a long time since the last break, tension is high among staff members in March. Be prepared.

True Story

> The beautiful little purple crocus that pokes its head through the snow welcomes a forthcoming spring in the north. It also signals a round of griping and complaining by parents and teachers. It has nothing to do with high-stakes testing.
>
> I could explain these behaviors away because skiing was over and golf and tennis hadn't started yet. People were suffering from cabin fever after usually long winters.
>
> Then, I moved to the south where the sun always shines, and I knew that the Crocus Syndrome would not exist. Guess what? No crocus, no snow, and still March signaled a round of griping and complaining by parents and teachers. Go figure!
>
> —Middle school grade level chair

How can you help teachers and students get through this testing month?

- Recognize the problem out in the open. Staff members need to be reminded that their attitudes are infectious. Students and colleagues need upbeat behavior. Laugh about how cranky teachers look and sound. Laugh at yourself, and laugh with each other.

- Last-minute pep talks should go to the teachers. They need to recognize that the importance of the tests cannot be overlooked but should "lighten up" with the students. By now, there is no student who doesn't get it that they need to do their best.

- Have very well-organized procedures for teachers to follow regarding their testing assignments, room arrangements, and monitoring schedules. Last-minute adjustments and changes drive teachers crazy when they are already feeling the stress of high-stakes testing.

- Unfortunately, teachers also need a reminder that if the protocol of the test is not followed as prescribed, they can lose their jobs. It seems odd that some teachers don't understand that concept, but many don't and need reminding.

Learning Continues in Spite of Testing

Chapter 8 described the concerns that arise when teachers believe students are too tired to learn anything else while the tests occur. It is important for you to reinforce your expectations that dispel the myth. Let it be known that you expect meaningful, focused learning to continue during testing time.

You may need to get very creative in working with staff to ensure this is possible. If students are displaced to another room and another teacher is monitoring the test, how disrupted is the day's schedule for all students and teachers?

There is good news! Spring break usually occurs around this time. You can catch your breath; teachers and students will leave you alone. You can now work on the budget.

The Budget: March and April

Review program and model costs.

- ◆ Did student progress justify the expense of staff, materials, and supplies for unique programs? On what basis did you draw those conclusions?

- ◆ Project enrollment carefully. Cautiously evaluate a peak in enrollment when you must complete your budget projections. Use data from one year to the next to evaluate population-enrollment trends over time.

- ◆ Discuss the budget with others. Work with your mentor, coach, and other principals to find out what they would recommend or what they are doing. You don't have to follow their ideas, but it is helpful to get others' thoughts. When you go to your supervisor with your budget, you will have a thorough basis of understanding about your requests.

- ◆ Every district gives principals different levels of control over their budgets. For districts with significant central office control, you don't have much wiggle room. Judge what you can or cannot do before you get carried away with your projections in your "perfect world." Your discretionary money may be pretty limited. Just know what you are doing with what you will receive.

Staff Reappointment, or Not: April—Or, Before Spring Break, the Time Finally Comes

Just before spring break, call the staff together for a meeting and lay out the plans that you and your School Improvement Planning Team determined to focus on for the upcoming year. All of your hard work is finally coming to fruition. You spent most of the year gathering data and creating your philosophical position and vision. You collaborated with key leaders in the school to provide direction. You observed teachers and drew your own conclusions regarding the potential of each teacher to support the plan. Now is the time to let the staff know that there is a plan.

You and your team will lay it out. Why now? It helps teachers know, before you reappoint staff members to their positions, whether they can help the school grow. If you lay out the plan before spring break, it gives teachers time to think about what they want to do. This is the time to give teachers the option of whether they want to return to work under the plan or not. You may have teachers who want to go somewhere else because they can't live with your expectations. Cut them loose.

You have teachers you will ask to leave, even if they want to stay. Teachers will give you a commitment to work with the school plan, when really they have no intention of changing their existing strategies. By now, you have figured that out. Cut them loose.

It is hard to replace a big chunk of your teachers after your first year, but don't beat yourself up over it. It is not uncommon to take two or three years to stabilize a staff with faculty who believe in the school's philosophy and vision.

It is almost easier to start with someone new than to retrain a philosophical dinosaur. For the tenured staff member who is digging in his or her heels or whom you can't or won't get rid of, refer to Chapter 7 for strategies.

The following form is an example of one to use when getting insight into the staff member's intent to return.

The School Planning Team and I have completed the process of clarifying the school philosophy and vision that will remain our focus at _____ School. As discussed at our staff meeting, the philosophy and vision are as follows: _____

_____

Please complete the following:

Teacher name: _____ Date: _____

Current teaching assignment: _____

I have read and heard the philosophy and vision statement. I would like to become a part of the direction the school is going. I plan on returning to the school next year.

Yes_____ No _____

My choice of class or grade level is as follows:

First choice: _____

Second choice: _____

Third choice: _____

This information will provide another piece of documentation to use when meeting with the teacher for his or her final evaluation.

Relapse: April and May

Chapter 8 discussed the issue of lost instructional time in the school. The problem seems to get even worse after spring break. Testing and spring break are over. Students and teachers start counting the days until summer. It is hard to keep everyone on track. You are tired and just want the year to end so that you can start over with a year for which you are better prepared.

Assume that it is around the first of April, and you end school in May. School won't be over for about two months, eight weeks, 40 days, or 240 instructional hours. (But who is counting? You get the idea regardless when your school year ends). There is an upcoming year for which to prepare students.

How to Keep the Focus

- This is a time to bring teams of teachers together and get a collective second wind. Emphasis should be on the remaining meaningful instruction—with "meaningful" being the operative term.
- Students also need a shot in the arm to stay focused. Discuss with teams how they plan to keep students learning.
- Even though you are swamped at this time of the year, maintain your observation schedule and continue to look at lesson plans.
- Teachers need to understand that next year's assessment begins the day after this year's assessment—a concept that isn't often discussed. Principals are so busy, and teachers know that and often wind down their instruction much sooner than necessary. Staff members are well aware that the principal or administrative staff won't have time to observe them.

Learning Until the Last Day of School

Surprise the staff—model the importance of learning until the last day of school—and continue going into classrooms. Go back to the note form you used at the beginning of the year (see Chapter 6) and leave notes on the teacher's desk. Let teachers know you are still interested in what is happening until the last day of school. Use the same strategy you used earlier in the year.

File the notes to be used for the next school year. Staff members need to understand that caring about their individual instruction does not occur only from September through March or April.

Another issue occurs when teachers who know they are either moving classrooms or moving out of the school start packing up their personal supplies well before the end of the school year. This puts the younger students off balance. It seems like a simple thing, but students need the same structure to stay focused. Walking around boxes during the last weeks of school sends quite a message from the teacher: "I'm out of here." What incentive does that give students to continue learning?

Elementary teachers have so much stuff that they, too, create an off-balance classroom atmosphere if they start dismantling their classrooms weeks before school is over. Middle and high school students "zone out." Students need structure until the last day. This is a message that you should make clear: Dismantle the room after students are gone at the end of the year, and not until.

The Master Schedule

Assessing students' academic needs for the upcoming year is another complex process that varies from elementary, middle, and high schools. Some solutions are possible, others are not. However, some considerations should be examined.

- ◆ Elementary school
  - Some principals ask teachers to create an individual profile for each student that tells their academic level in reading and math. They also identify each child's behavioral issues. In this way, assignments are made, in most schools, to provide a heterogeneous arrangement. In other schools, assignments are made on the basis of academic achievement and place students according to the school model.
  - After the initial placement by teachers, the principal, guidance counselor, English for speakers of other languages teachers, and exceptional education teachers preview the placements to make sure students are assigned according to the children's needs.
  - The final step occurs when the principal and assistant (if there is one) arrange the students for the final balance of classrooms. At this point, decisions are based on the philosophy and vision for the students.
  - Another consideration is the quality of this year's teacher. If a student had a fragmented year because of teacher absenteeism,

division of classrooms during the year, or a poor-quality teacher, then you want to ensure the next teacher is strong. You are the only one who can make that decision.

- Be prepared for parent requests. Often, a sibling had a successful experience with Ms. Smith and the parent wants the same teacher. Somehow, Ms. Jones is known to have all the "good, smart" kids, so the parent wants that teacher. What was your predecessor's policy? Was there one? What will you establish as your policy? Make sure you clearly define the parameters for accommodating parents. Once you make an exception—and you probably will—look out because word spreads. Ask your mentor for suggestions.

- ◆ Middle school
  - Middle school student placement is generally determined by the student's previous teacher, profile, tests, and assessments.
  - Guidance counselors often go to the feeder elementary schools to gather data from teachers about entering middle school students.
  - Students are assigned based on the model the school uses, such as students in specific integrated teams, advanced track, track for special needs students, or a totally heterogeneous model.
  - Parent requests often become problematic; be prepared for how you plan to handle this issue.

- ◆ High school
  - Student placement in high school courses becomes exponentially more complex as the school provides more offerings and as the school becomes larger.
  - Students are placed initially based on the school's class registration form, which is generally drive by a computer program.
  - Student and parent requests, tests, and assessments come into play. How do you plan to accommodate special requests?
  - Assign a responsible person, usually an assistant principal, to spend the weeks necessary to work through this maze of organization. The one who creates the master schedule must be talented in logic, puzzle-solving, and problem-solving skills. Hold on to your hat, this is one bumpy ride.

The domino effect when producing a large middle or high school's master schedule is enormous. As principal, it is up to you to provide the initial guidelines. First, classes built on the philosophy and vision of the school should drive the master schedule. For example, you and the staff believe that for learning and instruction to improve, more students should enter Advanced Placement classes (greater inclusion). Therefore, the master schedule should begin with an increase in Advanced Placement classes.

Naturally, every teacher's needs come to the front. Talk about crabby—now you will know what crabby looks and sounds like. Why? Just a few possibilities are identified here to prepare you for the onslaught.

- Classroom teachers want every planning period to attach to their lunch schedule for a longer lunch.
- Coaches, band, and drama teachers want the last period of the day for their planning period so they can prepare for games, events, performances, or practice after school gets out.
- New moms want the first period for their planning period in case of early-morning emergencies getting the baby ready for the day.
- Special interest classroom teachers—orchestra, creative writing, and drama—worry that the emphasis on putting more students in Advanced Placement will conflict with the same students enrolling in their classes.

June and July

The difference between last year and this year is your level of experience. Several areas will become clearer to you.

- Interviewing for next year will be easier. You now know the quality of teacher you want for the school. You know the teacher leaders who may help in the interview process. The focus of your questions will be the philosophy and vision of the school, with the teacher as the key to its success. You know the type of teachers necessary to support the School Improvement Plan.
- Test scores will be less confusing to interpret (unless the format and method of reporting has changed). You already have the last two year's data analyzed; now you just have one year to use for the comparison.
- The master schedule will reflect the philosophy and vision that you and the School Improvement Team developed.
- You know the vision but were not able to implement much during the first year.

- You know more about what you don't know. As a result, you will set about developing a plan to increase your knowledge, particularly in areas of unfamiliar curriculum.

Questions and Answers

Q: Why establish the School Improvement Plan during January when there is so much information that could be gathered later on in the year.

A: The School Improvement Plan is complex and can be addressed in parts. January simply addresses a chunk of the information concerning where the school is functioning at this point and provides an opportunity to gather the stakeholders and develop a direction. It is the one time of the year that is less hectic. Every month after January, it becomes harder to find the concentrated time needed.

- Remember, you run a school on a fiscal calendar, not a school calendar.
- You already have two years worth of data from which to draw conclusions.
- This is an opportunity to focus on new programs or models adopted from your predecessor's leadership; study their effectiveness.
- Part of your plan should create "what if" scenarios. Generally, test scores aren't available soon enough to gather a group that can focus on this year's testing issues.
- It is possible to gather a School Improvement Planning Team meeting in shorter time frames for issues that remain unresolved during the day of planning.

Q: How much impact can I expect to make as I begin my second year?

A: Honestly, just a little. You may make some cosmetic changes and act decisively on issues of health and safety in the first year. You begin with baby steps. You identify a core group that is on the same page; assign them the job of "infecting" others with the philosophy and vision of the school. Don't be impatient. It takes time and focus. You will continue to hone your skills needed in your school through the second year. It will start to come together during your third year, you will make real progress in the fourth year, and you will gain acceptance by the majority of the staff in the fifth year.

Q: I am passionate about a particular model for instruction that I believe is a must for my school. It improved test scores in my old school. But it's a new idea and wasn't being implemented at the school when I took over. I want to put it into place for the second year. What steps should I take?

A: Don't take any steps. Stop. Think smart. As brilliant an idea as you may have, you have not gained the trust of or developed credibility with the staff, even after your first year. Anything you introduce as a new idea should wait. Methodical and thoughtful baby steps are needed for any idea to take hold. Spend your time and energy understanding the issues presented in this and other chapters in this book. The slow turtle wins the race. Your time will come. Be patient.

 **Survival Tips**

Learn how to organize, facilitate, and process a School Improvement Plan. Take advantage of any opportunity prior to assuming a principal or assistant principal role to participate in the school planning process—not as a way to identify specific goals and objectives for an individual school, but to watch and learn the process of organizing, facilitating, and processing the information that drives the school for the upcoming year.

When in doubt, get them out. As difficult as it may be to replace an ineffective teacher, do it. If you do not see noticeable improvement in a new teacher during the course of the year, it probably won't happen. If a new teacher does not get along with others, it won't happen. A tenured teacher just takes longer. Do it.

Focus on your purpose, philosophy, and vision. Understanding your own purpose, philosophy, and vision provides you the focus and clarity necessary to lead a school. Your ability to collaborate with staff to develop a common philosophy and vision for the school gives you the road map by which to travel. Under your leadership, shared decision making places ownership of the school's progress with the stakeholders. The success of the students and staff becomes everyone's commitment.

Know how to create a master schedule based on the school philosophy and vision.

Establish your credibility in a variety of ways.

- Your personal sense of what will make the school great

- Your ability to provide the necessary support identified in the School Improvement Plan and to understand of staff needs
- Complete documentation concerning what you observed about a teacher's interaction with others and his or her classroom effectiveness
- Your ability to clearly, firmly, and empathetically use that information in the evaluation of a teacher
- Your ability to communicate the school philosophy and vision because you are clear about what you want an effective school to demonstrate

Authority is granted to you based on your position, but power is earned. The adage states, "Authority is granted by your superordinates, power is granted by your subordinates." It isn't the authority that makes a leader—that is given to you with the position. You can hire and following the proper guidelines, you can fire staff. You can manage the school budget and require adherence to district policies. In other words, there is no need to throw your weight around to prove you are the boss. This just asks for a contentious, nonproductive environment.

Power is granted to you by those with whom you work, lead, and manage. Power is earned. You are given power by the staff in a variety of ways. Usually, power comes when teachers believe that you are credible, trustworthy, supportive, empathetic, and any other characteristics the culture of the school values.

Listen. You may not want to hear what a staff member has to say, but listen before you make a decision. Only life-threatening issues require a quick or negative response to those concerns brought to your attention. Make an informed decision instead of an emotionally charged one.

Understand the difference between decisiveness and arrogance. Everyone knows what the sign on your desk that says "principal" means. You don't need to prove it just because you can. Some issues are simply nonnegotiable because of required policies and procedures. Staff members need to know the nonnegotiable issues and why they are nonnegotiable.

Barking "no" at a staff member just because you have the authority to do so does not win a loyal staff. If the answer to a request is no, then it is worth your time and the respect due the teacher to explain the rationale behind the decision. Take time to discuss the issue.

During your first year on the job, you don't need a reputation as a tyrant instead of leader.

Don't ask the question if you don't want the answer.

- If the issue, generally management in nature, is a matter of just making a decision, then do it.

- It doesn't take a committee to know what to do when the fire alarm goes off.

- If you have already made up your mind on an issue and nothing will convince you otherwise, then don't ask the question. It takes staff members about five minutes to figure out that you asked them what they thought, with their expectation that their opinions counted, and your mind was already made up. The result is that the next time you ask for staff member's opinions, you only get grumbling. "Why should we bother, she will do it the way she wants anyway."

Avoid last-minute hires at all costs. Staff members who announce they are leaving the school with only a couple of weeks left before school starts go with the territory, frustrating as it is. At that time, you are faced with a dilemma: Do you hire a substitute to start the year and pray you find someone later? Or, do you find anyone who can walk and chew gum at the same time just to get someone in the classroom? Last-minute hires are a huge problem.

- Good teachers get hired fast. Begin the process of interviewing as soon as possible. Check with your mentor to determine how to recruit early and hire the best candidates.

- If you have no choice, last-minute hires and those hired during the year need lots of extra support as quickly as possible.

Conscientiously check a potential teacher's past history. Some teachers are very charismatic and interview well. When it is hard to find good teachers, you and your team can be easily charmed into offering a position before you call a candidate's previous employer or references. Huge mistakes could occur as a result of overzealous hiring.

High-growth areas are especially hard hit in trying to employ new teachers. It is not uncommon for a candidate to try to pressure an interviewer into making a quick decision because "I have already been offered a position at school X and I am suppose to let them know my decision today." Be careful, it could be a ploy. After checking credentials, this candidate may not meet your standards.

Summary

The last months of school create challenges on two levels. On one level, you are working with a plan developed by your predecessor and his or her team. This gave you time to begin learning the culture of the school.

Then, after the winter holiday break, you began putting your leadership skills to the test. Now you will begin leading for next year as you set in motion the wheels that will drive the school.

There are important preliminary steps that must be secured before you have a firm foundation for your home. What is your passion about the success you want for the teachers and students?

- ◆ Define who you are: What makes you tick? Why are you in the education business? *What is your purpose?*

- ◆ How does that purpose drive your *philosophical belief*—the belief that encompasses the totality of your hopes and dreams for the school?

- ◆ What is your *vision* for how your passion and plans for the teachers and students will come to fruition?

- ◆ How will you create a *collaborative community*—that is, a school community in which you do not try to be the boss of everything, but where you are willing to make hard decisions when necessary. Allow those around you to assume leadership roles as you mentor and coach them, creating a school family with everyone who wants to grows and become successful.

The School Improvement Planning process is important because it provides a way for key members of the staff to work with you in establishing a clear and concise point of reference. Using a methodical problem-solving process with a collaborative approach gives an avenue of focus for the school.

School Improvement Planning Team members receive specific documentation from student assessments and program needs. You also will analyze information provided by teachers who implemented programs or models new to the school. As part of your role, you ensure that all data needed to make informed decisions becomes available to the team members.

You will influence many decisions because you know the nonnegotiable issues required by federal, state, and local requirements. However, you serve as a team member and model the importance of shared decision making. When minutes of meetings are distributed to the staff, everyone stays informed.

Evaluations of staff are based on clear, specific documentation that you compile throughout the year. Final evaluations reflect reappointments based on a teacher's competence, demonstration of student learning, commitment to the philosophy and vision of the school, and ability to work collaboratively with others.

Reappoint only those teachers who will help move the school forward. You show your decisiveness when you won't accept anyone but the best. If you cannot dismiss a teacher, then find him or her a position that will least hinder student progress.

Although teachers know the importance you place on "doing well" on standardized tests, you are not neurotic about it. You reduce the stress on teachers and students as much as possible. You make it clear to students and teachers that there is life during and after testing. Learning continues throughout the year.

You model your expectation that students and teachers still have a job to do—preparing students for next year, even if that next year is the real world after graduation. You continue to visit classrooms, commenting on instruction while supporting teachers and students.

You review carefully the cost compared to the effectiveness of programs and models when you prepare the budget. You analyze trends in population growth or reduction over the last three years. The trend line provides realistic expectations concerning the number of students projected to attend school for the upcoming year.

Because the majority of money is spent on teachers' salaries, you work methodically to determine how best to stretch the remaining money provided. You methodically identify the number of teachers and teaching positions that will be necessary for the upcoming year.

Careful interviewing of teachers may require others from the proposed team or department to assist in the interview process. You know the type of teacher you want to move the school forward. Accept only the best.

Reflections

1. Refer to the beginning of this chapter and identify the purpose, philosophy, and vision that reflect your beliefs. Put each in writing. Compare your responses to those of your teammates. What are the commonalities? What makes your beliefs different?

2. Locate a decision-making and problem-solving model. Study the methods and strategies used by identifying a problem that exists in your school. It may be a single issue or a problem that could come to the School Improvement Team. With a team member, demonstrate how the model works and critique its effectiveness.

3. Identify a program or model that your school implemented during the last two years. Develop a format with the accompanying

information to describe the program or model, the population it served, and its effectiveness.

4. Create a profile of a fictitious mental dinosaur in your school. Identify the subject area and hypothetical issues that the person who appears to lack any desire to follow the School Improvement Plan might exhibit. List the steps necessary to determine what to do and how to do it. What are the problems that you might encounter when making your decisions?

5. Assume that you have been assigned to a school that is considered *traditional*. You know that students must have more than skills in order to function. They need to learn to think at higher levels. You are almost through with your first year at the school. As you review the opportunities over the year to "infect" the staff with your beliefs, what would you do, when would you do it, and how would you do it? Hypothetically, what barriers might exist? How might you overcome them? Discuss your ideas with a team member or write your plan.

6. What issues most affect the master schedule at your existing school? What do you want to drive the master schedule? Why?

Conclusions

The learning curve during your first year on the job was pretty steep, wasn't it? You experienced a lot, didn't you?

What You Probably Learned

The best part of the job—energy boosters:

- Solving problems
- Watching and learning from great teachers
- Seeing improvement in students and teachers
- Interacting with the school community
- What would you add?

The hardest part of the job—energy drainers:

- Crabby parents with persistent agendas
- High-maintenance teachers
- Dismissal of teachers
- Crisis and major conflicts
- Not knowing what to worry about—so you worried about everything
- What would you add?

Looking forward to next year:

- Analyzing data with a clearer understanding of how to draw conclusions
- Understanding my personal purpose, philosophy, and vision

- Expanding the circle of teacher leaders with whom I work as we collaboratively move the philosophy and vision forward
- Coaching struggling and new teachers and helping them to improve
- Learning and studying more issues of curriculum, instruction, and assessment
- What would you add?

The surprises:

- I was not able to build my vision to the extent I expected.
- I spent more time analyzing my observations of the culture than I had expected.
- Not everyone loves me.
- I couldn't get everything done that I thought I could as quickly as I had expected.
- It was hard to discipline myself to get into classrooms every day, all year, but it made such a difference in my credibility and understanding of what was going on around the school.
- My job is less about managing and more about collaborating. I thought I could just be the boss. It isn't about that.
- Although I am managing, I am first and foremost the instructional leader.
- What would you add?

The Next Steps

At this point, you can frame your purpose, philosophy, and vision and put it on your desk to remind you of your focus. In this way, when the demands of your job fragment your day, you can continuously remind yourself of how to continue moving the school forward.

You Gain Some Time during the Summer

Each of the steps you completed this year will be repeated again for next year and the year after that, with some exceptions. You can eliminate the intense interviewing of each group because you already know enough information by now about job responsibilities and individual insights about the school. Time saved: three to four weeks.

Take a break and refocus your energy. It is unlikely that you took much time off during your first year. There was so much to do—and you had to *study* the school, not just *run* the school—that you didn't know what you didn't have to do, so you did everything. Now you know how to better prioritize. You know which of your staff can be depended on to accomplish the tasks you assign. During the three weeks you gained by eliminating the interviewing, you need to become reenergized. Do it.

Where Is Your School Going?

Now that you have a minute to collect your thoughts, reread the School Improvement

Plan. Will the plan actually move the school forward? Or is the plan so focused on improving test scores that it doesn't actually meet your vision? You recognize that eventually you want a whole-school reform. Yet that notion could not be a part of the School Improvement Plan because all teachers wouldn't know what you are talking about, and it requires a longer time frame to implement.

Where does your long-range vision, including the one that you developed collaboratively with the staff, fit in next year? Summer is the time to think that piece through.

Take advantage of *think time* during the summer. You can now look at the new standardized test scores and compare them to last year's. Draw additional conclusions. Did anything new appear? If so, what will you do with the information?

Review yearly lesson plans from selected teachers (in large schools, it is too time-consuming to review everyone's) and evaluate any additional documentation that may help you to study the improvement of teachers and students. In this way, you can determine just how far the staff can advance during the upcoming year.

Review your final assessments of selected teachers. This also gives you the opportunity to assess marginal teachers whom you reappointed. You can identify the issues you want to bring to their attention first thing in the school year with an individual teacher plan. Start early with a formal plan.

You may want to adjust the members of the Leadership Team to bring aboard teachers who can provide you the most support. If possible, find the money to gather those teachers together for a retreat. After your experience last year, you know how to organize, establish a meaningful agenda, and develop strategies of which you now have ownership. You will feel much more comfortable in this setting after one full year of living in the culture.

You will realize your collective vision if you approach every step by working *smart, hard,* and *efficient*. Maintain your focus and hold firm to your purpose and philosophy. For the sake of the school, stay there for the consistency that schools need over time. The following timelines may put into perspective the long-term commitment that is necessary for the staff to eventually internalize the philosophy and vision of the school.

Year 2: All of the planning, studying, and thinking begin to pay off. This year, teachers no longer wonder what you are all about. You begin making baby steps toward progress.

Years 3 and 4: The majority of your staff will begin to understand where the school is heading. Some teachers will still be leaving, but the majority that stay will be your greatest advocates.

Years 5 to 8: Under your leadership, the philosophy and vision will entrench themselves. Bringing your vision to fruition is a long-term commitment on the part of all stakeholders. It takes time and patience. It takes focus and the ability to remain firm in your resolve to best serve the needs of the students regardless of the inevitable resistance. Take strength from those who understand the vision and demonstrate its value in the classroom. Over time, more and more teachers will join you. You will win over the large majority of them.

Whatever shape your culture takes under your guidance, higher-order thinking, problem solving, and decision making are the primary guiding principles and the constant skills for principals, teachers, and students. This can be accomplished in a collaborative environment that exemplifies a student-centered focus. Your passion for your vision will prevail.

Appendix A

The Overwhelmed Administrator: This Can Occur at Any Time to Anyone— Recognize It!

Avoidance Behaviors

Procrastinating with excuses such as

- "Tomorrow I'll get it done for sure."
- "I'm too tired to think about it today."
- "I forgot."
- "I can't remember where I put the (form/directions/information). It's in a file somewhere, or maybe one of these piles."

Finding an issue and "beating the poor dead horse to death," taking hours longer than necessary on concerns for which there is no resolution.

Disappearing on campus. (Your car is still in the parking lot.) Finding hiding places where no one knows where you are.

- Where none of the agreed-upon signals work ("Oh, was that for me?")
- Walkie-talkie ("I forgot to turn it on").
- Search teams can not locate you. ("Were you looking for me? I must have just missed you.")

Leaving campus without letting anyone know where you are.

- "I just ran to the store to get something for lunch."
- Creating a nonexistent meeting to attend. "The meeting was cancelled; the traffic was terrible. I knew that by the time I got back to school it would be so late that I just went home."
- "My cell phone battery died."

Concentrating on the nonessential issues to avoid getting into classrooms during student–teacher contact time.

- "I need to look at some catalogues for a file cabinet."
- "I'm going to the discount store for some new flowers for the front of the school."
- "I have to get that dead tree (that has been dead forever) taken care of this week."
- "I need to see where the custodial closets are located."

Studying the test scores again. (Thinking, "If I stare at them long enough, I am will figure something out and the scores will improve.")

Staring at nothing in particular. ("There is a glazed look in my eyes.")

Fixating on the computer screen. ("Just how long can I look at those fish swimming on the screen saver?")

Hanging out, visiting for the sake of visiting, with anyone.

- Discovering that if you hang out with the food service staff, you can kill a lot of time and get free food in the process.

**Tackle one piece of information at a time. Focus.
If you find yourself engaging in these behaviors—stop!**

Appendix B

10 Big Ones: Key Survival Tips

The following survival tips are not ranked in order of importance nor in chronological order according to the chapters. Rather, each of the items is embedded within the portions of the book, and each one is significant.

- ◆ Develop a relentless schedule that gives you daily access to several classrooms and a variety of exchanges with staff—with no excuses.
- ◆ Reflect continuously on the purpose, motivation, and driving forces that brought you to the principal or assistant principal job.
- ◆ Review your personal and academic perspective and its potential effect on your interactions with others.
- ◆ Develop a methodical approach to solving problems in a collaborative environment (you are not in this alone).
- ◆ Manage your time.
- ◆ Learn from the experts around you.
- ◆ Support others and help them grow; remain empathetic.
- ◆ Study the data and make decisions based on facts and teacher discussions.
- ◆ Keep the total school in mind.
- ◆ Hire and keep only the best faculty who know their craft and cooperate with you and their colleagues.

Recommended Reading

Ackerman, D. (2003). Taproots for a new century: Tapping the best of traditional and progressive education. *Phi Delta Kappan, 84*(5), 344–349.

Ackerman, R., Donaldson G., & Van Der Bogert, R. (1996). *Making sense as a school leader: Persisting questions, creative opportunities.* San Francisco: Jossey-Bass.

Adler, M. (1977). *Reforming education.* New York: Macmillan.

Alvy, H. B., & Robbins, P. (1998). *If I only knew…Success strategies for navigating the principalship.* Thousand Oaks, CA: Corwin Press.

Apple, M., & Beane, J. (1995). *Democratic schools.* Alexandria, VA: Association for Supervision and Curriculum Development.

Aslett, D. (1994). *The office clutter cure: How to get out from under it all.* Pocatello, ID: Marsh Creek Press.

Association for Supervision and Curriculum Development. 1995. *Toward a coherent curriculum* (1995 Yearbook). Alexandria, VA: Author.

Association for Supervision and Curriculum Development. 1989. *Toward the thinking curriculum: Current cognitive research* (1989 Yearbook). Alexandria, VA: Author.

Bamburg, J., & Andrews, R. (1990). School goals, principals, and achievement. *School Effectiveness and School Improvement, 2,* 175–191.

Barnard, C. I. (1938). *The functions of the executive.* Cambridge, MA: Harvard University Press.

Barth, R. (1990). *Improving schools from within.* San Francisco: Jossey-Bass.

Barth, R. (2001). *Learning by heart.* San Francisco: Jossey-Bass.

Bell, L. I. (2003). Strategies that close the gap. *Educational Leadership, 60*(4), 32–34.

Bellah, R., Madsen, R., Sullivan, W., Sidler, A., & Tipton, S. (1985). *Habits of the heart.* New York: Harper & Row.

Bennis, W. (1989). *On becoming a leader.* Reading, MA: Addison-Wesley.

Bennis, W., & Nanus, B. (1985). *Leaders: The strategies for taking charge.* New York: Harper & Row.

Benson, G. (1992). Chaos theory: No strange attractor in teacher education. *Action in Teacher Education, 14*(4), 61–67.

Bereiter, C. (1985). Cognitive coping strategies and the problem of inert knowledge. In J. W. Chipman & R. Glaser (Eds.), *Thinking and learning skills* (Vol. 2, pp. 65–80). Hillsdale, NJ: Lawrence Erlbaum.

Berger, K. S. (1978). *The developing person.* New York: Worth Publishers.

Berk, L. E., & Winsler, A. (1995). *Scaffolding children's learning: Vygotsky and early childhood education.* Washington, DC: National Association for the Education of Young Children.

Berlak, A., & Berlak, H. (1981). *Dilemmas of schooling: Teaching and social change.* New York: Methuen.

Berman, P., & McLaughlin, M. (1978). *Federal programs supporting educational change* (Vol. 8). Santa Monica, CA: RAND Corporation.

Bernard Powers, J. (1999). Composing her life: Hilda Taba and social studies history. In M. S. Crocco & O. L. Davis (Ed.), *Bending the future to their will: Civic women, social education, and democracy* (pp. 189–192). Lanham, MD: Rowman & Littlefield.

Birchak, B., Connor C., Crawford, K. M., Kahn, L., Kaser, S., Turner, S., & Short, K. G. (1998). *Teacher study groups: Building community through dialogue and reflection.* Urbana, IL: National Council of Teachers of English.

Black, S. (2000, September). Finding time to lead. *American School Board Journal.*

Blais, D. (1988). Constructivism—A theoretical revolution for algebra. *Mathematics Teacher, 81,* 624–631.

Blase, J., & Blase, J. (1998). *Handbook of instructional leadership: How really good principals promote teaching and learning.* Thousand Oaks, CA: Corwin Press.

Blase, J., & Kirby, P. C. (2000). *Bringing out the best in teachers: What effective principals do* (2nd ed.). Thousand Oaks, CA: Corwin Press.

Bloor, D. (1974). *Knowledge and social imagery.* London: Routledge/Kegan Paul.

Bodrova, E., & Leong, D. (1996). *Tools of the mind: The Vygotskian approach to early childhood education.* Columbus, OH: Merrill.

Bolman, L., & Deal, T. E. (1997). *Reframing organizations: Artistry, choice, and leadership* (2nd ed.). San Francisco: Jossey-Bass.

Boud, D. (1991). *The challenge of problem-based learning.* New York: St. Martin's Press.

Bowsher, J. (1989). *Educating America: Lessons learned in the nation's corporations.* New York: Wiley.

Bransford, J. D. (1989). New approaches to instruction: Because wisdom can't be told. In S. Vosniadou & A. Ortony (Eds.), *Similarity and analogical reasoning* (pp. 470–497). New York: Cambridge University Press.

Bransford, J. D., Brown, A., & Cocking, R. (2000). *How people learn: Brain, mind, experience, and school.* Washington, DC: National Academy Press.

Brimijoin, K., Marquissee, E., & Tomlinson, C. A. (2003). Using data to differentiate instruction. *Educational Leadership, 60*(5), 70–73.

Brookover, W., Beady, C., Flood, P., Schweitzer, J., & Wisenbaker, J. (1979). *School social systems and student achievement: Schools can make a difference.* New York: Praeger.

Brooks, G., & Brooks, M. G. (1993, 2000). *In search of understanding: The case for constructivist classrooms.* Alexandria, VA: Association for Supervision and Curriculum Development.

Brooks, G., & Brooks, M. G. (1999). The courage to be constructivist. *Educational Leadership, 57*(3), 18–24.

Brown, A., & Campione, J. C. (1994). Guided discovery in a community of learners. In K. McGilly (Ed.), *Classroom lessons: Integrating cognitive theory and classroom practices* (pp. 229–270). Cambridge: MIT Press.

Brown, J. L., & Moffett, C. A. (1999). *The hero's journey: How educators can transform schools and improve learning.* Alexandria, VA: Association for Supervision and Curriculum Development.

Bruner, J. (1971). *The relevance of education.* New York: WW Norton.

Burbules, N. C. (2000). Moving beyond the impasse. In D. C. Phillips (Ed.), *Constructivism in education: Opinions and second opinions on controversial issues* (pp. 308–330). Chicago: University of Chicago Press.

Burns, J. M. (1978). *Leadership.* New York: Harper & Row.

Caine, G., Caine, R. N., & Crowell, S. (1999). *Mindshifts: A brain compatible process for professional development and the renewal of education.* Tucson, AZ: Zephyr Press.

Caine, R. N., & Caine, G. (1991). *Making connection: Teaching and the human brain.* Alexandria, VA: Association for Supervision and Curriculum Development.

Caine, R. N., & Caine, G. (1997). *Education on the edge of possibilities.* Alexandria, VA: Association for Supervision and Curriculum Development.

Carpenter, W. (2000). Ten years of silver bullets: Dissenting thoughts on educational reform. *Phi Delta Kappan, 81*(5), 383–389.

Carr, J. F., & Harris, D. E. (2001). *Succeeding with standards: Linking curriculum, assessment, and action planning.* Alexandria, VA: Association for Supervision and Curriculum Development.

Cawelti, G. (1984). Behavior patterns of effective principals. *Educational Leadership, 41*(5), 3.

Chittenden, E., & Gardner, H. (1991). Authentic evaluation and documentation of student performance. In V. Perrone (Ed.), *Expanding student assessment* (pp. 22–31). Alexandria, VA: Association for Supervision and Curriculum Development.

Clark, D. L., & Austuto, T. A. (1994). Redirecting reform: Challenges to popular assumptions about teachers and students. *Phi Delta Kappan, 75*(7), 513–520.

Cochran Smith, M., & Lytle, S. (1990). Research on teaching and teacher research: The issues that divide. *Educational Researcher, 19*(2), 2–11.

Collins, J. (2001). Good to great. New York: HarperCollins.

Colvin, S. (1911). *The learning process.* New York: Macmillan.

Combs, A., Miser, A., & Whitaker, K. (1999). *On becoming a school leader: A person-centered challenge.* Alexandria, VA: Association for Supervision and Curriculum Development.

Confrey, J. (1990). What constructivism implies for teaching. In R. Davis (Ed.), *Constructivist views on the teaching and learning of mathematics* (p. 109). Reston, VA: National Council of Teachers of Mathematics.

Conley, S., &. Bacharach, S. (1990). From site management to participatory school site management. *Phi Delta Kappan, 17*(7), 539–544.

Corbett, H. D., Dawson, J., & Firestone, W. (1984). *School context and school change.* New York: Teachers College Press.

Costa, A. (2000). Getting into the habit of reflection. *Educational Leadership, 57*(7), 60–64.

Costa, A., & Kallick, B. (2000). *Habits of mind: Discovering and exploring.* Alexandria, VA: Association for Supervision and Curriculum Development.

Cottrell, V. (2005). Ventures for excellence. *Lincoln, NE: Ventures for Excellence.*

Covey, S. R. (1991). *Principle-centered leadership.* New York: Fireside.

Crandall, D., Eiseman, J., & Louris, K.(1986). Strategic planning issues that bear on the success of school improvement efforts. *Educational Administration Quarterly, 22*(3), 21–53.

Crawford, M., & Whitte, M. (1999). Strategies for mathematics. *Teaching in Context, 57*(3), 34–38.

Cunningham, W. (1993). *Cultural leadership: The culture of excellence in education.* Boston: Allyn & Bacon.

Daft, R. L., & Lengel, R. H. (2000). *Fusion leadership: Unlocking the subtle forces that change people and organizations.* San Francisco: Berrett Koehler.

Daggett, W. R. (2001, June 24). *The 21st century classroom: A new focus on learning.* Keynote address presented at the Ninth Annual Model Schools Conference, Orlando, FL.

Danielson, C. (2002). *Enhancing student achievement: A framework for school improvement.* Alexandria, VA: Association for Supervision and Curriculum Development.

Daresh, J. D. (2001). *Beginning the principalship: A practical guide for new school leaders* (2nd ed.). Thousand Oaks, CA: Corwin Press.

Darling-Hammond, L. (1997). *The right to learn: A blueprint for creating schools that work.* San Francisco: Jossey-Bass.

Davenport, L. (2001). *Order from chaos: A 6-step plan for organizing yourself, your office, and your life.* New York: Three Rivers Press.

Deal, T. E., & Peterson, K. D. (1999). *Shaping school culture.* San Francisco: Jossey-Bass.

Dewey, J. (1900). *The school and society.* Chicago: University of Chicago Press.

Dewey, J. (1966). *Democracy and education.* New York: Free Press.

Dixon, R. (1994). Future schools and how to get there from here. *Phi Delta Kappan, 75*(5), 360–366.

DuFour, R., & Eaker, R. (1998). *Professional learning communities at work: Best practices for enhancing student achievement.* Bloomington, IN: National Educational Service.

Duke, D. (1982). Leadership functions and instructional effectiveness. *National Association of Secondary School Principals, 66,* 5–9.

Dweck, C. (1991). Motivation. In A. Lesgold & R. Glaser (Eds.), *Foundation for a psychology of education* (pp. 87–136). Hillsdale, NJ: Lawrence Erlbaum.

Dweck, C., & Legget, E. (1988). A social cognitive approach to motivation and personality. *Psychological Review, 95,* 256–273.

Eggen, P., & Kauchack, D. (1997). *Educational psychology: Windows on classrooms* (3rd ed.). Upper Saddle River, NJ: Merrill.

Eisenberg, R., & Kelly, K. (1997). *The overwhelmed person's guide to time management.* New York: Penguin.

Eisner, E. W. (2002). The kind of schools we need. *Phi Delta Kappan, 83*(8), 576–583.

Eisner, E. W. (2003). Questionable assumptions about schooling. *Phi Delta Kappan, 84*(9), 648–685.

Elias, M., Zins, J., Weisserg, R., Frey, K., Greenberg M., & Haynes, N., et al. (1997). *Promoting social and emotional learning.* Alexandria, VA: Association for Supervision and Curriculum Development.

Elmore, R. F. (1995). Getting to scale with good educational practice. *Harvard Educational Review, 66*(1), 1–26.

Elmore, R. F., & Furhman, S. H. (2001). Holding schools accountable: Is it working? *Phi Delta Kappan, 83*(1), 67–70, 72.

Ennis, R. H. (1996). *Critical thinking.* Upper Saddle River, NJ: Prentice Hall.

Erickson, H. (2001). *Stirring the head, heart, and soul: Redefining curriculum and instruction* (2nd ed.). Thousand Oaks, CA: Corwin Press.

Evans, R. (1996). *The human side of school change.* San Francisco: Jossey-Bass.

Fein, A. (2003). *There and back again: School shootings as experienced by school leaders.* Lanham, MD: Scarecrow Press.

Felier, R. (2000). Teachers leading teachers. *Educational Leadership, 57*(7), 66–69.

Finser, T. M. (1994). *School as a journey: The eight-year odyssey of a Waldorf teacher and his class.* Hudson, NY: Anthrosophic Press.

Firestone, W. (1989). Using reform: Conceptualizing district initiative. *Educational Evaluation and Policy Analysis, 11*(2), 151–164.

Firestone, W., & Corbett, H. D. (1987). Planned organizational change. In N. Boyand (Ed.), *Handbook of research on educational administration* (pp. 321–340). New York: Longman.

Fleck, F. (2005). *What successful principals do! 169 tips for principals.* Larchmont, NY: Eye on Education.

Fogarty, R. (1997a). *Brain-compatible classrooms.* Arlington Heights, IL: Skylight.

Fogarty, R. (1997b). *Problem-based learning and other curriculum models.* Arlington Heights, IL: Skylight.

French, J. P., & Raven, B. (1959). The bases of social power. In D. Cartwright (Ed.), *Studies in social power.* Ann Arbor: University of Michigan, Institute for Social Research.

Friedin, N., & Slater, M. R. (1994). School leadership and performance: A social network approach. *Sociology of Education, 67,* 139–157.

Fullan, M. G. (1991). *The new meaning of educational change.* New York: Teachers College Press.

Fullan, M. G. (1996). What's worth fighting for in your school? *New York: Teachers College Press.*

Fullan, M. G. (1997). *The challenge of school change: A collection of articles.* Arlington Heights, IL: Skylight.

Fullan, M. G. (1999). *Change forces: The sequel.* Philadelphia: Falmer Press.

Fullan, M. G. (2001). *Leading in a culture of change. San Francisco: Jossey-Bass.*

Gabriel, J. G. (2005). *How to thrive as a teacher leader.* Alexandria, VA: Association for Supervision and Curriculum Development.

Gagnon, G., &. Collay, M. (2001). *Designing for learning: Six elements in constructivist classrooms.* Thousand Oaks, CA: Corwin Press.

Gardner, H. (1991). *The unschooled mind: How children think and how schools should teach.* New York: BasicBooks.

Gardner, H. (1999). *The disciplined mind: What all students should understand.* New York: Simon & Schuster.

Garmston, R. (1995). Adaptive schools in a quantum universe. *Educational Leadership, 52*(7), 6–14.

Giuliani, R. (2002). *Leadership.* New York: Miramax.

Glatthorn, A. A. (1994). *Developing a quality curriculum.* Alexandria, VA: Association for Supervision and Curriculum Development.

Glickman, C. D., & Gordon, S. (2001). *Supervision and instructional leadership: A developmental approach.* Needham Heights, MA: Allyn & Bacon.

Goleman, D. (2000). *Working with emotional intelligence.* New York: Bantam Books.

Goodlad, J. (1984). A place called school. *New York: McGraw-Hill.*

Goodlad, J. (1994). *Educational renewal: Better teachers, better schools.* San Francisco: Jossey-Bass.

Goodlad, J. (1996). Sustaining and extending educational renewal. *Phi Delta Kappan, 78*(3), 228–234.

Gordon, S. P. (2000). *Professional development for teacher and school renewal: Alternative pathways, common characteristics.* Paper presented at the University Council for Educational Administrators' Annual Convention, Albuquerque, NM.

Greenberg, J. (1990). *Problem-solving situations: A teacher's resource book* (Vol. 1). New York: WW Norton.

Greenleaf, R. K. (1977). *Servant leadership.* New York: Paulist Press.

Griffith, J. (2000). School climate on group evaluation and group consensus: Student and parent perception of the elementary school environment. *Elementary School Journal, 101*(1), 35–61.

Guiney, E. (2001). Coaching isn't just for athletes: The role of teacher leaders. *Phi Delta Kappan, 82*(10), 740–743.

Gunter, H. (1997). Chaotic reflexivity. In M. G. Fullan (Ed.). *The challenge of school change: A collection of articles* (pp. 87–114). Arlington Heights, IL: Skylight.

Guskey, T. R. (2000). *Evaluating professional development.* Thousand Oaks, CA: Corwin Press.

Hall, G., & Hord, E. (2001). *Implementing change: Patterns, principles, and potholes.* Needham Heights, MA: Allyn & Bacon.

Hallinger, P., & Murphy, J. (1987). Assessing and developing principal instructional leadership. *Educational Leadership, 44*(1), 54–61.

Hargreaves, A. (1994). *Changing teachers, changing times.* London: Cassell.

Hargreaves, A. (1997). Rethinking educational change. In M. G. Fullan (Ed.), *The challenge of school change: A collection of articles* (pp. 1–26). Arlington Heights, IL: Skylight.

Hargreaves, A. (1998a). The emotional policies of teaching and teacher development: Implications for educational development. *International Journal of Leadership in Education, 4,* 315–336.

Hargreaves, A. (1998b). *What's worth fighting for out there?* New York: Teachers College Press.

Hargreaves, A., & Dean, F. (2000). The three dimensions of reform. *Educational Leadership, 67*(7), 30–33.

Harvey, D., & Brown, D. (2000). *An experiential approach to organization development.* Upper Saddle River, NJ: Prentice Hall.

Hayes-Jacobs, H. (1989). *Interdisciplinary curriculum: Design and implementation.* Alexandria, VA: Association for Supervision and Curriculum Development.

Hemphill, B. (2002). *Taming the paper tiger at work.* Washington, DC: Kiplinger.

Hodgkinson, C. (1991). *Educational leadership, the moral art.* Albany: State University of New York Press.

Huberman, M. (1990). *The social context of instruction in schools.* Washington, DC: American Educational Research Association.

Huberman, M., &. Miles, M. (1984). *Innovation up close.* New York: Plenum.

Isaacson, L. S. (1993, 1994). *Classrooms of the 21st century: The busy educator's guide.* Orlando, FL: Orange County Public Schools.

Isaacson, L. S. (2004). *Teachers' perceptions of constructivism as an organizational change model: A case study.* Unpublished doctoral dissertation, University of South Florida, Tampa, FL.

Jensen, E. (1998). *Teaching with the brain in mind.* Alexandria, VA: Association for Supervision and Curriculum Development.

Johnson, D., & Johnson, R. (1989). *Leading the cooperative school.* Edina, MN: Interaction.

Kanter, R. M. (1989). *When giants learn to dance.* Simon & Schuster.

Katzenmeyer, M., & Moller, G. (1996). *Awakening the sleeping giant: Leadership development for teachers.* Thousand Oaks, CA: Corwin Press.

Knapp, M. (1995). Academic challenge in high poverty classrooms. *Phi Delta Kappan, 76,* 770–776.

Kohn, A. (1998). *What to look for in classrooms.* San Francisco: Jossey-Bass.

Kohn, A. (1999). *The schools our children deserve.* Boston: Houghton Mifflin.

Kouzes, J. M., & Posner, B. Z. (1987). *The leadership challenge: How to get extraordinary things done in organizations.* San Francisco: Jossey-Bass.

Kralovec, E., & Buell, J. 2000. *The end of homework: How homework disrupts families, overburdens children and limits learning.* Boston: Beacon Press.

Lambert, L. (2003). *Leadership capacity for lasting school improvement.* Alexandria, VA: Association for Supervision and Curriculum Development.

Lambert, L., Walker, D., Zimmerman, D., Cooper J., Lambert, M., Gardner, M., & Slack, P. (1995). *The constructivist leader.* New York: Teachers College Press.

Lampert, M., &.Ball, L. (1999). Multiples of evidence, time, and perspective: Revising the study of teaching and learning. In E. Lagemann & L. S. Shulman (Eds.), *Issues in education research: Problems and possibilities* (pp. 374–398). San Francisco: Jossey-Bass.

Lee, V. (1993). The organization of effective secondary schools. In L. Darling Hammond (Ed.), *Review of research in education* (pp. 171-267). Washington, DC: American Educational Research Association.

Lewin, L., & Shoemaker, B. (1998). *Great performances: Creating classroom-based assessment tasks.* Alexandria, VA: Association for Supervision and Curriculum Development.

Lieberman, A. (1996). Forward. In A. Lieberman (Ed.), *The series on school reform* (pp. ix–x). New York: Teachers College Press.

Lieberman, A., & Miller, L. (1990). Restructuring schools: What matters and what works. *Phi Delta Kappan, 71*(10), 759–764.

Liontos, L. B. (1994). *Shared decision making.* Eugene, OR: ERIC Clearinghouse on Educational Management. (ERIC Document Reproduction Service No. ED368034)

Littkey, D., & Grabelle, S. (2004). *The big picture: Education is everyone's business.* Alexandria, VA: Association for Supervision and Curriculum Development.

Little, J. W. (1982). Norms of collegiality and experimentation: Workplace conditions of school success. *American Educational Research Journal, 19,* 325–340.

Lortie, D. (1975). *Schoolteacher: A sociological study.* Chicago: University of Chicago Press.

Louis, K. (1990). *Improving the urban high school: What works and why.* New York: Teachers College Press.

Luttrell, W. (2000). "Good enough" methods for ethnographic research. *Harvard Educational Review, 70*(4), 497–523.

Malen, B., Ogawa., R. T., & Kranz, J. (1990). What do we know about school-based management: A case study of the literature a call for research. In W. H. Clune & J. F. Witte (Eds.), *Choice and Control in American Education: Vol. 2. The practice of choice, decentralization and school restructuring* (pp. 289–342). New York: Falmer Press.

Manz, C., & Sims, H. (2001). *The new superleadership.* San Francisco: Berrett Koehler.

Marzano, R. (2003). *What works in schools: Translating research into action.* Alexandria, VA: Association for Supervision and Curriculum Development.

Marzano, R., Pickering, D., & Pollock, J. (2001). *Classroom instruction that works.* Alexandria, VA: Association of Curriculum Development.

Maslow, A. H. (1954). *Motivation and personality.* New York: Harper & Row.

Mattessich, P. (1992). *Collaboration: What makes it work.* St. Paul, MN: Amherst H. Wilder Foundation.

Maxwell, J. C. (1995). Developing the leaders around you. *Nashville, TN: Thomas Nelson.*

Maxwell, J. C. (2001). *The 17 indisputable laws of teamwork.* Nashville, TN: Thomas Nelson.

McEwan, E. (2003). *10 traits of highly effective principals: From good to great performance.* Thousand Oaks, CA: Corwin Press.

McLaughlin, M., & Pfeiffer, R. S. (1988). *Teacher evaluation: Improvement, accountability, and effective learning.* New York: Teachers College Press.

Merriam, S. B. (1998). *Qualitative research and case study applications in education.* San Francisco: Jossey-Bass.

Miller, J. (2001). *QBQ! The question behind the question.* Denver, CO: Denver Press.

Moffett, C. (2000). Sustaining change: The answers are blowing in the wind. *Educational Leadership, 57*(7), 35–38.

Morgan, D. A. (1997). Focus groups as qualitative research. *Thousand Oaks, CA: Sage.*

Muncey, D. (1993). Preliminary findings from a five-year study of the coalition of essential schools. *Phi Delta Kappan, 74*(6), 486–489.

Napier, R. W., & Gershenfeld, M. K. (1999). *Groups, theory, and experience* (6th ed.). Boston: Houghton Mifflin.

National Association of Elementary School Principals. (2002). *Standards for what principals should know and be able to do.* Alexandria, VA: Author.

National Board for Professional Teaching Standards. (2001). Leading from the classroom. *Accomplished Teacher Magazine* [Online]. Retrieved August 20, 2003 from xxx.

National Board of Professional Standards. (2003). *Education reform: Why America needs NBCTs.* Retrieved from www.nbpts.org/edreform/why.cfm.

National Research Council. (2000). *How people learn: Brain, mind, experience, and school.* Washington, DC: National Academy Press.

Newman, D. P., Griffin, P., & Cole, M. (1989). *The construction zone: Working for cognitive change in school.* New York: Cambridge University Press.

Newmann, F. (1995). *Authentic pedagogy and student performance.* San Francisco: American Educational Research Association.

Nicholls, A., & Reschke, C. (1993). *Education as adventure: Lessons from the second grade.* New York: Teachers College Press.

Nolen-Larson, J. (1999). *Coping with loss.* Mahwah, NJ: Lawrence Erlbaum.

Norris, S., & Ennis, R. (1989). *Evaluating critical thinking.* Pacific Grove, CA: Critical Thinking Press.

Northwest Regional Educational Laboratory. (1984). *Effective schooling practices: A research synthesis.* Portland, OR: Author.

Ohanian, S. (2001). News from the test resistance trail. *Phi Delta Kappan, 82*(5), 363–366.

Ohanian, S. (2003). Capitalism, calculus, and conscience. *Phi Delta Kappan, 84*(10), 736–747.

Owens, R. (1998, 1995). *Organizational behavior in schools.* Needham Heights, MA: Prentice Hall.

Palmer, P. J. (1998). The courage to teach. *San Francisco: Jossey-Bass.*

Peacock, J., & Holland, D. (1988). *The narrated self: Life stories and self construction.* Symposium on self-narrative presented at the American Anthropological Association, Phoenix, AZ.

Perkins, D. (1992). *Smart schools: From training memories to educating minds.* New York: Free Press.

Perrone, V. (1991). *Expanding student assessment.* Alexandria, VA: Association for Supervision and Curriculum Development.

Peters, T. (1987). Thriving on chaos. *New York: HarperCollins.*

Peters, T. (1994). *Tom Peters seminar: Crazy times call for crazy organizations.* New York: Vintage.

Pogrow, S. (1996). Reforming the wannabe reformers: Why education reforms almost always end up making things worse. *Phi Delta Kappan, 77*(10), 656–663.

Posner, G. J. (1992, 1995). Analyzing the curriculum. *New York: McGraw-Hill.*

Prestine, N., & McGreal, T. (1993). Benchmarks of change: Assessing essential school restructuring efforts. *Educational Administration Quarterly, 33*(3), 371–400.

Putnam, H. (1990). *Realism with a human face.* Cambridge, MA: Harvard University Press.

Reeves, D. (2004). *Accountability for learning: How teachers and school leaders can take charge.* Alexandria, VA: Association for Supervision and Curriculum Development.

Reigeluth, C. (1999). *Instructional design theories and models* (Vol. 2). Mahwah, NJ: Lawrence Erlbaum.

Resnick, L. (1989). *Toward the thinking curriculum: Current cognitive research.* Alexandria, VA: Association for Supervision and Curriculum Development.

Richardson, V. (2003). The dilemmas of professional development. *Phi Delta Kappan, 84*(5), 401–406.

Richardson, V., & LeFevre, D. (2000). Staff development and the facilitator. *Teaching and Teacher Education, 18,* 483–500.

Riechman, D. (2003, September 9). Bush puts focus on education plan. *Orlando Sentinel,* p. A21.

Robert Greenleaf Center for Servant-Leadership. (1995). *Reflections on leadership: How Robert K. Greenleaf's theory of servant-leadership influenced today's top management thinkers* (L. Spears, Ed.). New York: Wiley.

Roberts, D., &. Babinski, L. (1999). Breaking through isolation with new teacher groups. *Educational Leadership, 56*(8), 42–47.

Rosenholtz, W. (1989). *Teacher's workplace: A social-organizational analysis.* New York: Longman.

Saphier, J. (1985). Good seeds grow in strong cultures. *Educational Leadership, 42,* 67–73.

Sarason S. B. (1996). *Revisiting "The culture of the school and the problem of change."* New York: Teachers College Press.

Schein, E. H. (1985). *Organizational culture and leadership.* San Francisco: Jossey-Bass.

Scherer, M. (1999). The understanding pathway: A conversation with Howard Gardner. *Educational Leadership, 57*(3), 12–16.

Schlechty, P. C. (1990). *Schools for the 21st century.* San Francisco: Jossey-Bass.

Schlechty, P. C. (2001). *Shaking up the school house: How to support and sustain educational innovation.* San Francisco: Jossey-Bass.

Schön, D. (1971). *Beyond the stable state.* New York: WW Norton.

Schools Examination and Assessment Council (London Schools Curriculum and Assessment Authority). (1990). *Pack C. Vol. 38: A guide to teacher assessment.* London: Author.

Sellars, W. (1991). *Science, perception and reality.* Atascadero, CA: Ridgeview.

Senge, P. M. (1990). *The fifth discipline: The art and practice of the learning organization.* New York: Doubleday.

Senge, P. M. (2000). *Schools that learn: A fifth discipline fieldbook for educators, parents, and everyone who cares about education.* New York: Doubleday.

Sergiovanni, T. J. (1999). *Rethinking leadership.* Arlington Heights, IL: Skylight.

Shapiro, A. S. (2000). *Leadership for constructivist schools.* Lanham, MD: Scarecrow Press.

Shapiro, A. S. (2003). *Case studies in constructivist leadership and teaching.* Lanham, MD: Scarecrow Press.

Shelley, N. (1999, 2000). *The art of constructivist teaching in the primary school.* London: David Fulton.

Shields, P. (1997). The promise and limits of school based reform: A national snapshot. *Phi Delta Kappan, 79*(4), 288–294.

Shulman, L. (1989). Teaching alone, learning together: Needed agendas for the new reform. In T. Sergiovanni & J. Moore (Ed.), *Schooling for tomorrow: Directing reforms to issues that count* (pp. 166–187). Boston: Allyn & Bacon.

Shulman, L. (1999). Taking learning seriously. *Change, 31*(4), 11–17.

Sigel, O., & Hooper, F. H. (1968). *Logical thinking in children.* New York: Holt, Rinehart and Winston.

Sirotnik, K. (1999). Making sense of educational renewal. *Phi Delta Kappan, 80*(8), 606–610.

Sizer, T. (1992). *Horace's school: Redesigning the American high school.* Boston: Houghton Mifflin.

Slavin, R. (1990). *Cooperative learning theory, research, and practice.* Englewood Cliffs, NJ: Prentice Hall.

Smircich, L. (1983, September). Concepts of culture and organizational analysis. *Administrative Science Quarterly, 28*(3), 64–94.

Smith, K. K. (1989). The movement of conflict in organizations: The joint dynamics of splitting and triangulation. *Administrative Science Quarterly, 34,* 1–20.

Smith, L. (2001). Can schools really change? Charting the dimensions of substantial change efforts. *Education Week, 21,* 30, 32–33.

Smylie, M. A. (1997). Research on teacher leadership: Assessing the state of the art. In B. J. Biddle (Ed.), *International handbook of teachers and teaching* (pp. 521–577). Dordrecht, Netherlands: Kluwer Academic.

Snowden, P. E. (1998). *School leadership and administration: Important concepts, case studies, and simulations.* New York: McGraw Hill.

Soder, R. (1999). When words find their meaning. *Phi Delta Kappan, 80*(8), 568–578.

Stake, R. (1995). *The art of case study research.* Thousand Oaks, CA: Sage.

Streifer, P. (2001, April). Data driven decisions: New ways to get answers. *School Administrator, 58*(4).

Terrence, E. D., & Peterson, K. D. (1999). *Shaping school culture: The heart of leadership.* San Francisco: Jossey-Bass.

Trubowitz, S. (2000). Predictable problems in achieving large scale change. *Phi Delta Kappan, 82*(2), 166–168.

Tucker, P. D., & Stronge, J. H. (2005). *Linking teacher evaluation and student learning.* Alexandria, VA: Association for Supervision and Curriculum Development.

Vaill, P. B. (1984). The purposing of high-performing systems. In T. J. Sergiovanni (Ed.), *Leadership and organizational culture.* Urbana: University of Illinois Press.

Villani, C. J. (1996). *The interaction of leadership and climate in four suburban schools: Limits and possibilities* (Doctoral dissertation, Fordham University, 1996). (UMI No. 9729612).

Vygotsky, L. (1930). *Mind in society: The development of the higher psychological processes.* New York: Oxford University Press.

Weiss, C. (1993, Fall). Shared decision making about what? A comparison of schools with and without teacher participation. *Teachers College Record* 95(1), 69–92.

Wheatley, M. (1992). *Leadership and the new science: Learning about organization from an orderly universe.* San Francisco: Berrett Koehler.

Wiggins, G. (1993). *Assessing student performance: Exploring the purpose and limits of testing.* San Francisco: Jossey-Bass.

Wiggins, G., & McTighe, J. (1998). *Understanding by design.* Alexandria, VA: Association for Supervision and Curriculum Development.

Wilson, K. G., & Daviss, B. (1994). *Redesigning education.* New York: Teachers College Press.

Wiske, M. S. (1996). *Teaching for understanding: Linking research with practice.* San Francisco: Jossey-Bass.

Wolfe, P. (2001). *Brain matters: Translating research into classroom practice.* Alexandria, VA: Association for Supervision and Curriculum Development.

Wonycott-Kytle, A., & Bogotch, I. (1997). Reculturing assumptions, beliefs, and values underlying the process of restructuring. *Journal of School Leadership, 7*(1), 27–49.

Zemelman, S., Daniels, H., & Hyde, A. (1993, 1998). *Best practices: New standards for teaching and learning in America's schools.* Portsmouth, NH: Heinemann.

Zmuda, A., Kuklis, R., & Kline, E. (2004). *Transforming schools: Creating a culture of continuous improvement.* Alexandria, VA: Association for Supervision and Curriculum Development.